BOOTSTRAPPED

Tables of Contents

Author's Note

Thank you for taking the time to purchase and now read this book. Believe it or not, I never intended to write a book. As I transitioned into my 20s and moved out of my parents' house, I prioritized documenting everything I learned along the way. Doing this allowed me to accumulate content for this book and taught me how to press forward and enjoy the moment no matter what I'm going through.

The goal of this book is not to let you in on the tea in my life. The goal is to show you how I took control of my story in real time and used it to find happiness in the moment and reach my goals. To take it to the next level, I decided to share my story online. I call this concept "preselling your story." By preselling my story in real time, I naturally attracted people, opportunities, and clients into my life. Since they knew who I was and what I was doing, most people wanted to support me on my journey in various ways. Some of these ways included buying my products/services, following me online, and spreading the word to their network. This unique positive feedback loop slowly increased my chances of success as I reached more people.

Not only was I able to meet new people and attract business by preselling my story in real time, but I also was able to impact people. By sharing the good, bad, and ugly parts of my story online, I encouraged people to chase after their dreams and reclaim their lives. Doing this gave me the energy to show up on the days I felt like giving up. I knew other people were looking up to me and counting on me.

Hopefully, my experiences will inspire you to document your journey and have fun along the way as you work towards your goals. Oh yeah, and remember: You will be *unstoppable* when you recognize that you are in control of your life and everything you are experiencing is a part of your story.

Why Did I Write a Book?

Growing up, I've always enjoyed reading books deep into the night. Heck, I would even create my own books by going into our home office, grab some sheets of paper, and start writing.

I even went through a MASSIVE self-development phase during my sophomore year of high school. I would clear one 200-page book each week for an entire year.

I always loved reading, but I never imagined myself writing and publishing a book.

Back in high school, I managed to blow up on YouTube. Due to the nature of my videos, I ended up getting completely demonetized months later. For those who don't know what getting demonetized means, it means having ads completely removed from your videos. Ads is how I made money off YouTube. No ads equals no revenue.

This change forced me to look for other ways to make money both online and in person.

Throughout my junior and senior years of high school, I tried a variety of business ideas. To give you a glimpse of what I did, I've tried:

1) Creating a social media marketing agency

This failed because it was the trending side hustle at the time. There were so many people marketing their services, it was difficult to get in front of a decision-maker because I would've been the fifth person to approach them that week about this service.

If I could meet with the decision-maker, I would often get undercutted because someone else would do the same work cheaper.

2) Creating a Shopify store

I've created three different Shopify stores in the past. The first one flopped completely. The second one did alright. The third one actually got traction, but my partner and I ran into some issues.

We were running ads and were able to get it to $100/day. We sourced products from China, so it took between three to four weeks for the products to reach our customers.

Once the first orders started arriving to our customers, the items were either super low quality or broken from shipping. This forced us to refund everyone and take a massive loss.

We had the option to put in the work to make it a legitimate business, but I personally wasn't passionate about selling fish tank decorations. I didn't want to be known for that.

3) Real estate wholesaling

I've done a variety of side hustles during my high school years, but the last experience I want to share is my experience with real estate wholesaling.

If you don't know what real estate wholesaling is, I'll provide a brief explanation.

Usually, it starts with a homeowner who is unable to pay their mortgage or needs money really FAST. As a solution, they decide to sell their house.

Since these homeowners need money fast, going through a bank or realtor is not a good option, so they'll gravitate towards investors with cash.

Cash buyers are useful because they can close a deal within the same week, unlike banks (30–45 days).

As a wholesaler, my duty was to go out and find these distressed homeowners looking to sell their houses.

For example, if their home was worth $100,000, I could easily negotiate it down to $80,000 using the speed of cash as leverage.

Once I get that number settled and signed on a contract, I'll next take that contract and mark it up to my end investor at $90,000. He is still getting a deal because the property is worth $100,000.

Assuming due diligence goes well, at closing, the investor will pay me $90,000 for the property, and I'll keep my portion of $10,000, then pass the rest on to the homeowner.

This all sounds good on paper, but my first deal completely shifted my mindset on the business model. You see, the first distressed homeowner I spoke to (and almost made a deal with) was with a lady and her family in Atlanta, Georgia.

She needed to sell her house ASAP to move across the country to assist with her ill mother. After lots of going back and forth, I was able to negotiate them down enough to where I could get a nice payday and enough to where an investor would want to follow through.

When I brought the deal to my investor, he almost moved forward with it but wanted me to bring the price down a little more so he could make more of a profit.

Knowing the homeowner's situation, I did not feel comfortable or happy doing this. Sure, it would've been nice getting a $5,000 or $10,000 payday, but it wasn't worth it. It did not feel right selling my soul like that.

I ended up going to the homeowner and told her to just go through a realtor to get the most money out of her property. After that, I never touched real estate wholesaling again.

This experience specifically taught me that business is all about solving people's problems and making everyone happy. After this experience, I made a promise to myself to only work on businesses that are ethical and genuinely makes me happy.

During my senior year in high school, we had a project called Senior Project. This was a project that was a huge portion of our grade in English. As a joke, I wanted to create a business, so I went home and started brainstorming.

As I was looking through my YouTube analytics, I noticed that all of my viral videos were about some sort of trend at the time, so I decided to create a group chat that notifies content creators about trends. I called it Trend Watchers.

Long story short, I presented my idea and ended up getting a failing grade of 69. After that day, I threw the idea in the bin and proceeded to graduate high school.

Fast-forward to November 2019, I ended up buying a $2,000 self-development course, which changed my life and was amazing for someone fresh out of high school. I learned how to set goals, build personal values and standards, plus so much other stuff.

As I was going through this course and crafting my dream life, I wanted to start a business. I planned on launching the business on New Year's Day, January 1st, 2020.

I remember New Year's Eve 2019. It was around 7 or 8 at night, and I was ready to launch my new business. As I was organizing my Google Drive, I passed by the folder with my idea for Trend Watchers. I kept on scrolling and then had the feeling that I should go back and pursue that idea instead.

I thought about it for a second, then said screw it. I scrapped my plans for the new business I was going to launch and revived my old school project, Trend Watchers.

About ten minutes before the new year, I was able to

- Purchase trendwatchers.co (for $7)
- Get a website up
- Create Facebook ads
- Build a basic MVP

Right as we crossed into 2020, I said a prayer, turned my Facebook ads on, and went to sleep.

Believe it or not, the Facebook ads worked well, but there was an issue. Whenever people would join the group chat, they noticed they were the only ones there, so they left and requested a refund. This taught me the importance of having beta testers for both feedback and social proof.

To get these beta testers, I went on Reddit and was able to round up 100 beta testers for Trend Watchers. These beta testers provided tons of valuable feedback, and I honestly wouldn't be where I'm at without them.

Our community was hosted on Discord and it worked well, but as the weeks went by, we started running into some problems.

- People wanted to filter trends by categories
- They wanted trend charts
- Discord is still sorta like a group chat, so you had to scroll endlessly to see what was posted months ago

Plus lots of other issues.

The only way to solve these issues was to go out and build my own software. I can't code, so I decided to hire it out.

Then I ran into another problem. Hiring it out to a third-party firm isn't cheap either. I was getting quotes for $40k–$75k. This was money I didn't have at the time.

I next tried to go the capital-raising route. Thankfully, when I was doing real estate wholesaling, I had A LOT of investor contacts that I knew personally. I ended up pitching the idea to all of them, but they all said no.

I was about to give up until I saw there was one I didn't call yet. His name was Adam. As I called Adam, he took the time to look at my pitch deck and gave me a call the next day.

What he said forever changed the course of my life.

He said that no one was going to put their money on a 19-year-old with no start-up experience or previous results. The only way for me to make my idea a reality was with the assistance of family and friends who understood my work ethic. Or go all in myself.

After I was told this, I sat on it for about a day and then decided to go all in.

Let me tell you something. On previous unrelated projects where I've spent other people's money, it's easy to blow through it without a second thought.

But when you invest your own money into something, you'll really know when you've made the wrong decision. The loss hits ten times harder.

As you make your way through this book, I'm going to show you all of the wins, losses, and lessons I've learned from growing a tech start-up in my parents' basement at the age of 19.

I've spent the past three years documenting my entire journey and decided to compile it into a book. Hope you enjoy it and are able to get TONS of value out of it.

Why You Should Read This Book

Your life is a book, and YOU are the author.

From a very young age, I was able to understand that simple phrase. I wish I could tell you exactly when and how I figured it out, but I have no idea.

However, I have two key defining moments that I believe helped me learn that I am the author of my story at a young age.

Let's first rewind to when I was in the fifth grade. I was a troubled student who always knew how to make my way into the principal's office at least a few times a week. It got so bad that I was almost expelled from school, but one teacher wanted to give me a shot.

I was removed from my original fifth-grade class and placed in another teacher's fifth-grade class. I wish I could tell you precisely what she did, but this change caused me to improve my behavior significantly.

I made fewer visits to the principal's office, my grades were going up, and everything was improving. One afternoon, some of my classmates wanted to steal candy from the teacher's desk. After creating the plan and running it by the group, they proceeded towards her desk and took some candy as planned. I almost joined them but decided to bail out at the last minute.

Somehow, their operation was successful, and they did not get in trouble or caught.

Fast-forward a few days, I was trying to create a Facebook account to play Farmville. Since I was under 18, I needed to use one of my parents' emails to verify the account.

Luckily, I knew my mom's computer password, so I used her email and went to her inbox to retrieve the code. Unfortunately, I'm a curious soul, so I went through her inbox and saw an email thread from my teacher.

As I opened the email, my jaw dropped wide open. I forgot the exact words it said, but my teacher saw the entire operation of my friends and I planning and stealing the candy from her desk.

As I kept reading the email, she pointed out how I did an excellent job of walking away and taking the less popular route. Reading that sentence made me feel special and proud of myself. From that day forward, I promised myself always to do what felt right no matter how unpopular the alternative path may seem.

After realizing that, I started pulling my grades up, made new friends, and even took the number-one spot in the school for being good at math. My teacher and mom never mentioned that email to me, so it was a silent win that shifted my mindset early on.

Fast-forward to sixth grade, my life completely changed.

We moved from Gaston, South Carolina, to Marietta, Georgia. I HATED this move. I had to start my social life from scratch and was in an unfamiliar place.

As a way to express my anger, I started getting in trouble at school again. It got so bad that two weeks after the first day of school, I almost got expelled for fighting the school's resource officer. At this point, my parents pulled me out of school and decided to homeschool me again.

As I made this transition, I was assigned to see an anger management counselor. I saw her for a couple of weeks and eventually snapped out of it.

I remember looking around her office and asking myself, *What am I doing here?* I still had a lot of anger and negative energy built up inside of me, but I felt like it was fuel I was wasting. I felt like I was wasting this fuel by telling the counselor my problems and how I felt.

Now, there's nothing wrong with going to see a therapist or counselor, but I realize that I had potential I was wasting. I wanted to capitalize on this potential by using this excess energy toward productive things.

Once I made this click in my head at 12 years old, I quickly told the counselor what she wanted to hear so I could get out of the sessions and start putting my energy towards some sort of project or business.

Fast-forward ten years, I've been able to do the following by age 22:

- Become YouTube famous
- Reach over 100 million people across my personal brands
- Start a software company in my parents' basement and grow it to 10k users
- Become a writer for entreprenuer.com
- Write and publish a book
- Appear on TV and get lots of natural press
- Travel to 41/50 states

- Start doing public speaking consistently
- Play the pipe organ (self-taught)
- Grow a side hustle Instagram page to 100k followers in five months

Why did I tell you these two stories?

I told you these two stories because these were moments in my life where I learned how to listen to my heart, walk against the crowd, and learn how to focus my time, energy, and attention on a specific goal and achieve it.

These paradigm shifts that I had at a young age allowed me to realize that I am the author of my book.

As you read this book, you'll get a glimpse into three years of my life. At the start of 2020, I decided to go all in and take the leap into entrepreneurship. As I followed my heart and went against the crowd, not only did I write the next chapters in my life story, but I found happiness and success along the way by accident.

Happiness doesn't come from financial success.

It comes from having successful relationships with yourself, family, friends, God, plus so much more!

As you read about the things I discovered along my journey, ask yourself the following questions:

- Am I being the author of my life's story?
- Am I working towards things that bring me happiness?
- Am I constantly getting out of my comfort zone?

- What do all of my relationships look like?

There is no need to answer them now. Just plant these questions in the back of your head. Also, there's no need to finish this book cover to cover within a short period. Feel free to take your time and read the chapters as you feel inspired. These are all of the lessons I learned during my journey. I hope this book inspires you to presell your story online!

If you find anything valuable in this book, post a picture on your Instagram story and tag me @dejon_brooks! I'll repost it on my story!

Note: I documented my journey through Instagram. All of my posts have maxed-out captions, and this entire book is just a compilation of my Instagram posts. At the beginning of each chapter, I attached an image. This image shows you exactly which post that chapter came from. For the chapters without an image, those were the Instagram posts that never went live.

Anyways, I hope you enjoy this book!

Things I Learned During My Journey

The Wonders of Compound Interest

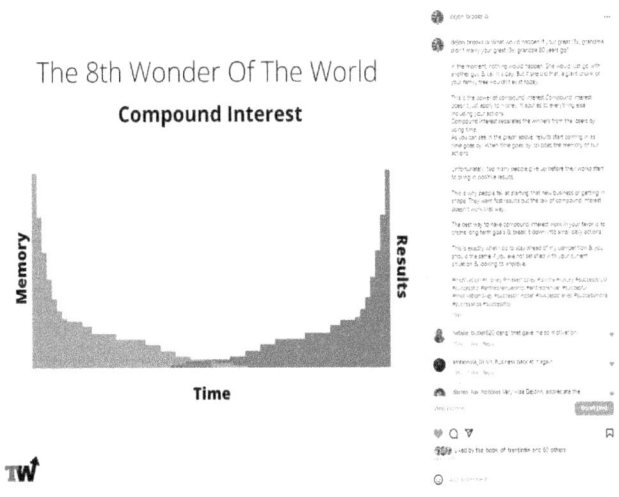

What would happen if your great-great-great-grandma hadn't married your great-great-great-grandpa eighty years ago?

At the moment, nothing would happen. She would go with another guy and call it a day. If that were the case, a giant chunk of your family tree wouldn't exist today.

This simple decision seemed harmless, but when you zoom out, it has a massive ripple effect. This is the power of compound interest. Compound interest doesn't just apply to money. It applies to everything else, including your actions.

Compound interest separates the winners from the losers by using time. As you can see in the graphic above, results start coming in as time goes by. When time goes by, so does the memory of our actions.

Unfortunately, too many people give up before their work starts to result in positive outcomes.

This is why people fail at starting that new business or getting into shape. They want fast results, but compound interest doesn't work that way.

The best way to have compound interest work in your favor is to create long-term goals and break them down into small daily actions.

I love focusing on small daily actions because it makes forgetting about the concept of time easier. When you take it a day at a time and enjoy the process, time will naturally fly by.

What happens when time flies by? Compound interest starts to work its magic.

This is exactly what I do to stay ahead of my competition, and you should do the same if you are not satisfied with your current situation and are looking to improve.

Found something valuable in this chapter? Share it by taking a picture and tagging me on your Instagram stories @dejon_brooks!

The Self-Improvement Equation

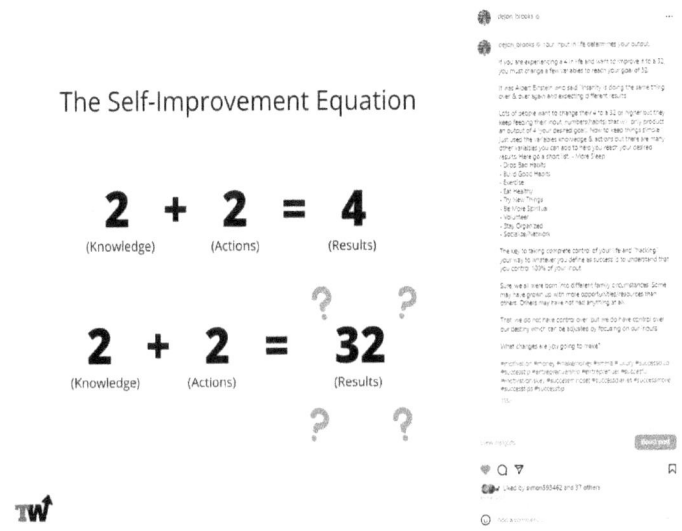

Your input in life determines your output.

If you are experiencing a 4 in life and want to improve it to a 32, you must change a few variables to reach your goal of 32.

Albert Einstein said, "Insanity is doing the same thing over and over again and expecting different results."

Many people want to change their 4 to a 32 or higher but keep feeding their input numbers (habits) that will only produce an output of 4 (your desired goal). Now, to keep things simple, I used the variables of knowledge and actions, but there are many other variables you can add to help you reach your desired results. Here is a short list:

- More sleep

- Drop bad habits

- Build good habits

- Exercise

- Eat healthy

- Try new things

- Be more spiritual

- Volunteer

- Stay organized

- Socialize/Network

The key to taking complete control of your life and "hacking" your way to whatever you define as success is to understand that you control 100% of your input.

Sure, we all were born into different circumstances. Some may have grown up with more opportunities/resources than others. Others may not have had anything at all.

We do not have control over that, but we do have control over our destiny, which can be adjusted by focusing on our inputs.

What changes are you going to make?

Why Motivation Sets You Up for Failure

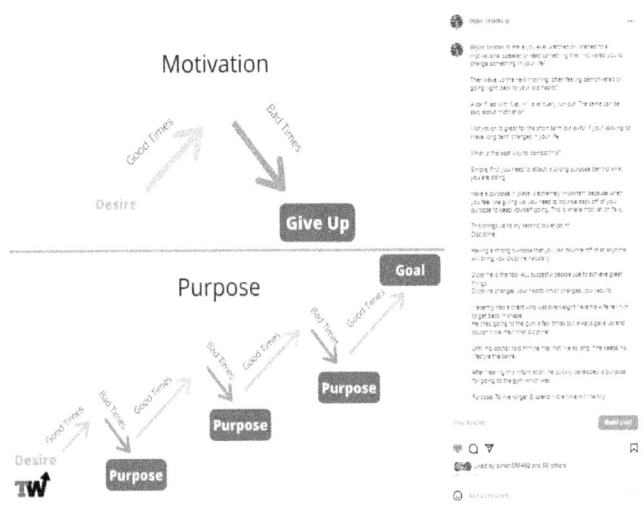

Have you ever watched or listened to a motivational speaker or read something that motivated you to change something in your life—then wake up the following day and return to your old habits?

As they say, a car filled with a full tank of gas will eventually run out. The same can be said about motivation.

Motivation is great for the short term but awful if you want to make long-term changes in your life.

What is the best way to combat this?

First, you must attach a strong purpose behind your actions.

Having a purpose in place is extremely important because when you feel like giving up, you can always bounce off your purpose to remind yourself of the long-term vision. This is great for keeping yourself going and is something motivation alone can't do for you.

Having a strong purpose you can bounce off of at any time will bring you discipline naturally.

Discipline is the tool ALL successful people use to achieve great things.
Discipline changes your habits, which changes your results.

I recently had a client who was overweight and had his wife tell him to get back in shape. He tried going to the gym a few times but always gave up and couldn't maintain that discipline.

It wasn't until his doctor told him he might not live long if he kept his current lifestyle. After hearing that, he quickly developed a purpose for going to the gym.

This purpose was to live longer and spend more time with family.

Also, this purpose quickly gave him the discipline to build a habit of regularly going to the gym.

After about three months of hard, persistent work, he lost a lot of weight and got his health back in order.

If you want to achieve something in your life, don't look for motivation to motivate you. First, seek a strong purpose that will give you the discipline needed to achieve whatever you want.

Initial Conditions

Initial Conditions

TW

Similar to habits, initial conditions are a concept that can make your life a whole lot easier or really hard.

It doesn't matter if it's a relationship, work, or how you manage time. Everything you do and interact with is affected by initial conditions.

For example, a tree tampered with within its early stages of growth will continue to grow that way for the rest of its existence. We see this often with plants placed in weird spots without sunlight. The plant will start to grow awkwardly towards any natural light it can get.

The same can be said about everything else in life. Issues present today, or issues that seem small, will only get bigger with time.

If you have spending issues making only $2,000 a month, your problems will only worsen when you get to $10k a month.

If you lie or steal a lot as an employee for a company, you'll still do the same thing as the CEO of that company.

Suppose your room or car is always messy. Slowly, other areas in your life (including your mind) will become chaotic and crowded.

This is why tackling problems early before time makes them worse is important.

Why is it important to understand initial conditions?

1. To understand that things won't magically fix themselves later. It would be best if you took action now.

2. You can use initial conditions with other people to find good people to associate with. If they start giving off red flags early on, the red flags will only increase with time. This is very common amongst dating, friendships, and people in general.

Even at work, people don't show up thirty minutes late out of the blue. It started by showing up right on time, being five minutes late, and so forth. They will only continue to push their limits if you don't say anything. It is essential to pay attention to the initial conditions of your relationships. Failure to do so can lead you you being taken advantage of.

3. Instead of letting negative attributes get bigger, you can change these to positive attributes for exponential personal growth.

Growing up, I had a lot of anger problems. By the time I reached middle school, it had gotten so out of hand I eventually got kicked out. If I didn't change my path quickly, my initial conditions with anger would lead me to spend most of my adult life in prison.

Because I was able to catch onto this and apply this energy towards something more productive, I've been able to scale this problem of mine in a positive way that impacts society.

Found something valuable in this chapter? Share it by taking a picture and tagging me on your Instagram stories @dejon_brooks!

Personal Foundations

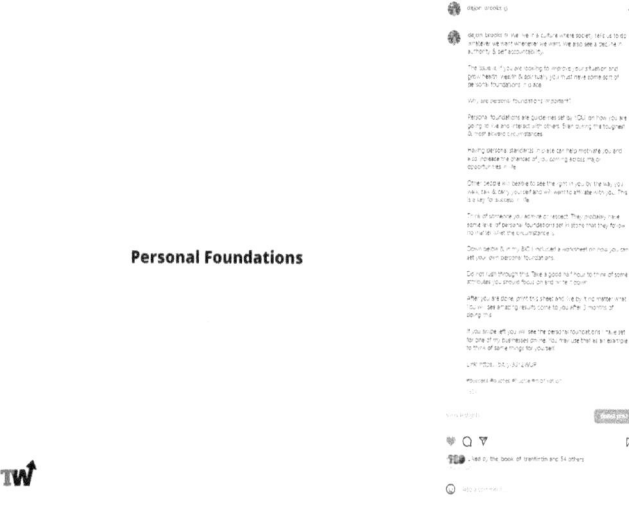

Personal Foundations

We live in a culture where society tells us to do whatever we want whenever we want. There are no consequences to our actions.

On top of this, there is a decline in personal values, religion, and self-accountability.

If you want to take your life to the next level and grow in the health, wealth, and spiritual departments, you must have some personal foundations.

Why are personal foundations necessary?

Personal foundations are guidelines set by YOU on how you will live and interact with others, especially during the most challenging circumstances.

Having personal standards in place can motivate you and increase the chances of coming across major life opportunities.

Other people will be able to see the light in you by how you walk, talk, and carry yourself, causing them to want to associate with you. This also prevents people from taking advantage and running over you.

Setting personal foundations for yourself is the key to living a happy, successful life.

Here are a few of the personal rules I've set for myself:

- Always go the extra mile
- Never take crap from anyone, and if you do, <u>know when to leave</u>
- Do EVERYTHING with passion
- There's always another bus coming in fifteen minutes
- Always take feedback head-on, both good and bad
- Never be the big fish in the room and stay there
- Always bring value to other people
- Do things today instead of tomorrow
- Always be closing
- Anything can be solved with a positive mindset
- Treat others the way I want people to treat me
- Track EVERYTHING

I have way more, but those are just a few of my favorite ones.

Now, here are some values I created for my start-up trendwatchers.co:

- **Be scientific.** We always test different ideas and listen to feedback to make better decisions.

- **Engage in long-term thinking.** We always sacrifice today for a better tomorrow.

- **Have a farmer's mentality.** We will plant 100 seeds and nurture them, hoping one will grow into something great.

- **Be data-driven.** We always make decisions based on previous data and information.

- **Be customer-obsessed.** We constantly enhance the quality of our service so our customers can get the best results.

- **Go against the crowd.** Don't be afraid to try something new.

These are both my personal and business operating rules, but take time to think about yours. Write them down on a piece of paper or a digital notepad.

There's no hurry; take half an hour or so to think of some attributes you should focus on.

After you are done, print your document and live by it. You will see amazing results after three months of doing this.

How to Spot Opportunities

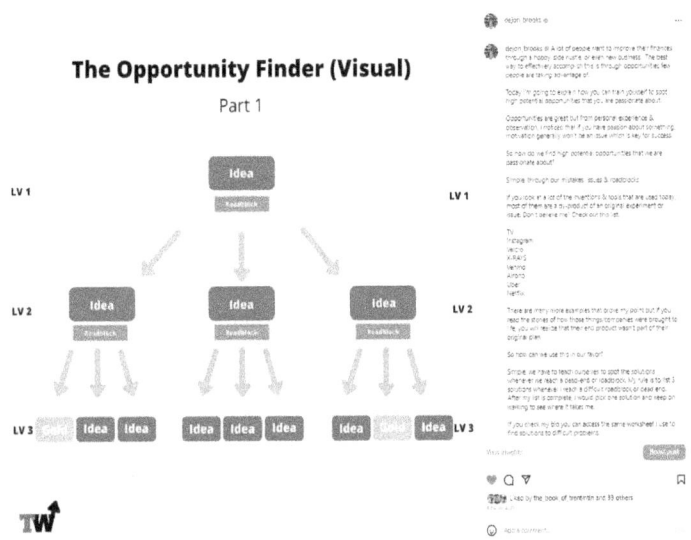

Many people want to improve their finances through a hobby, side hustle, or even a new business. The best way to accomplish this is through opportunities few people are taking advantage of.

In this chapter, I will show you how you can train yourself to spot high-potential opportunities you are passionate about.

Opportunities are great, but from personal experience and observation, motivation won't be an issue if you have passion for something. Being able to show up during the most challenging days is essential for success.

So, how do we find high-potential opportunities that we are passionate about?

Simple: through our mistakes, issues, and roadblocks.

If you look at a lot of the inventions and tools that are used today, most of them are a by-product of an original experiment or issue. Don't believe me? Pull out your phone and read how this list of items/companies was created:

- TV
- Instagram
- Velcro
- X-RAYS
- Venmo
- Airbnb
- Uber
- Netflix

Many more examples prove my point, but if you read the stories of how those things were brought to life, you will realize that their end product wasn't part of their original plan. It was an accident.

So, how can we use this in our favor? Well, the first thing you need to do is walk in one direction. It doesn't matter what direction it is. You need to start somewhere. Also, this somewhere might as well be something you love, so pick that.

Once you're heading in a specific direction, keep walking until you hit a dead-end or roadblock. Whenever I reach this point, I quickly pull out a pen and paper and list three solutions. Sometimes, I can list these solutions quickly, but other times, it may take me days or weeks. After completing my list, I would pick one solution and keep walking to see where it takes me.

The goal is to repeat this process until you find something that works. I like calling this method "digging for gold."

From my personal experience, these solutions can sometimes be massive opportunities in disguise that very few people are taking action on (that I'm passionate about!). Unfortunately, people today are looking for fast results, and when faced with a roadblock, most would dump the idea, say it doesn't work, and bounce to the next trendy idea.

The real opportunity is hidden 3–7 levels from the original idea, as shown in my visuals at the beginning of this chapter.

Did you find a roadblock?

Don't give up. Pull out a pen and paper and start brainstorming ways around it. I've solved some of the most IMPOSSIBLE problems using this method.

Found something valuable in this chapter? Share it by taking a picture and tagging me on your Instagram stories @dejon_brooks

Becoming Full Stack

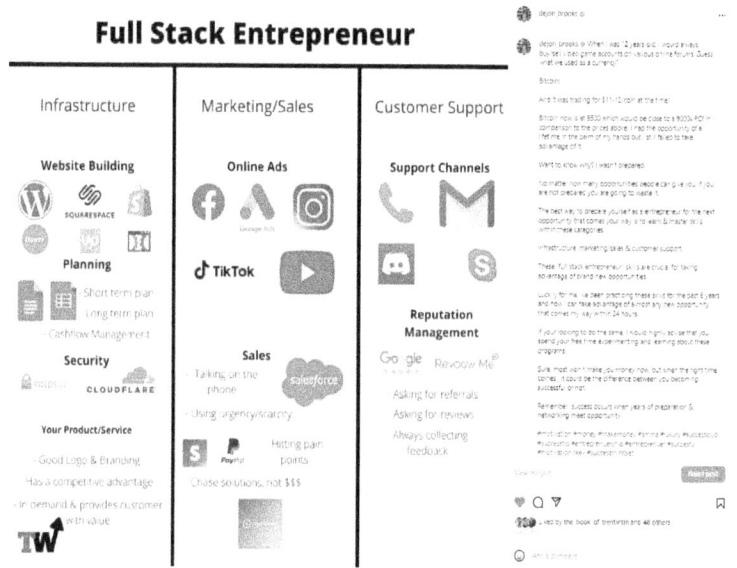

When I was 12 years old, I would always buy and sell video game accounts on various online forums. Guess what we used as a currency?

Bitcoin!

It was trading for $11-$12 a coin!

As of July 3rd, 2020, Bitcoin was at $9,500, which would be close to a 9000x ROI compared to the above prices. I had the opportunity of a lifetime in the palm of my hands, but I failed to take advantage of it.

Want to know why? I wasn't prepared.

No matter how many opportunities life gives you, you will most likely miss it if you are not prepared.

The best way to prepare yourself as an entrepreneur for the next opportunity that comes your way is to learn and master skills within a broad range of categories.

These categories include:

- Building infrastructure
- Marketing
- Sales
- Branding
- Customer support
- Fulfillment

These "full stack entrepreneur" skills are crucial for taking advantage of brand-new opportunities.

Luckily for me, I've been practicing these skills for the past six years, and now I can take advantage of almost any new opportunity that comes my way within twenty-four hours.

If you're looking to do the same, I recommend that you spend your free time experimenting and learning new skills. Especially skills you can stack with your current skill set.

When learning these skills, most won't make you money now. You'll often take a loss, but when the right time comes, it could be the difference between you becoming successful or not.

Remember, success occurs when years of preparation and networking meet opportunity.

Preventability

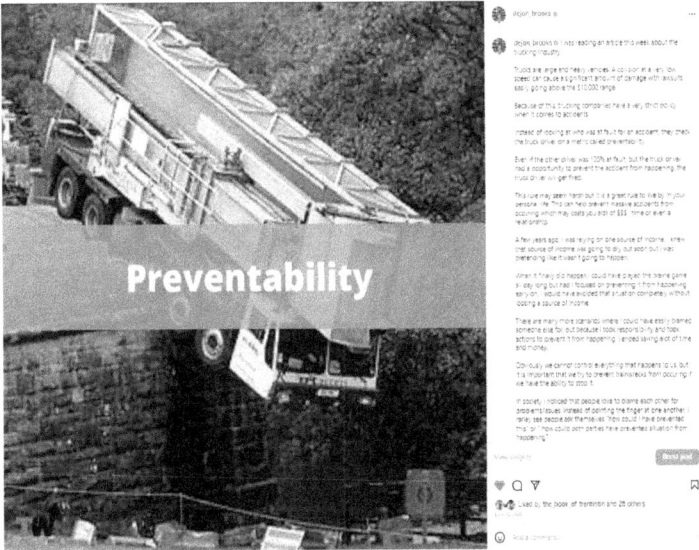

I was reading an article this week about the trucking industry.

Trucks are large and heavy vehicles. A collision at low speeds can cause significant damage, with lawsuits quickly going above the $10,000 range.

Because of this, trucking companies have a strict policy regarding accidents.

Instead of looking at who was at fault for an accident, they check the truck driver on a metric called preventability.

Even if the other driver was 100% at fault, if the truck driver had an opportunity to prevent the accident from happening, the truck driver could get fired.

This rule may seem harsh, but it is a great rule to live by, especially in your personal life. Being proactive instead of reactive can help prevent massive accidents, which may cost you a lot of money, time, or even a relationship.

A few years ago, I was relying on one source of income. I knew that source of income would dry out soon, but I pretended it wouldn't happen.

When it finally did happen, it temporarily put me in a tough patch in life. This rough spot could have been completely avoided had I taken action six months earlier.

We cannot control everything that happens to us, but we must try to prevent trainwrecks from occurring.

I noticed that people love to blame each other for societal problems. I rarely see people ask themselves, "How could I have prevented this?" or "How could both parties have prevented the situation from happening?"

If more people lived by this rule, the world would have less unnecessary chaos.

It also teaches you to take responsibility for your actions. This, combined with deep reflection, is key to growing as an individual.

Second-Order Consequences

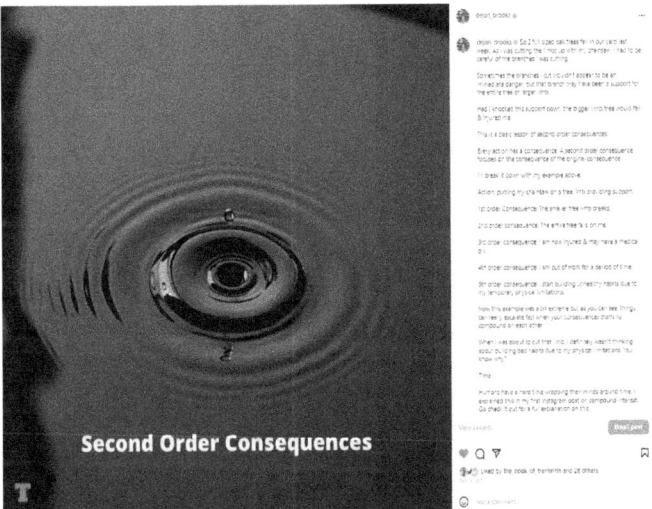

Two full-sized oak trees fell in our yard last week. As I was cutting the tree limbs with my chainsaw, I had to be careful with each cut I made.

Sometimes, the branches I was cutting wouldn't appear to be an immediate danger, only to find out it was a support for the entire tree or a larger limb I couldn't see.

Had I knocked this support down, the bigger limb or tree would have fallen and hurt me.

This is an introductory lesson on second-order consequences.

You see, every action has a consequence. A second-order consequence focuses on the consequence of the original consequence.

I'll break it down with some examples below.

Action: Putting my chainsaw on a tree limb provides support

1st-order consequence: The smaller tree limb breaks.

2nd-order consequence: The entire tree falls on me.

3rd-order consequence: I am now injured and may have a medical bill.

4th-order consequence: I am out of work for some time.

5th-order consequence: I start building unhealthy habits due to my temporary physical limitations.

This example was a bit extreme, but as you can see, things can escalate fast when your consequences compound each other.

Here is another one...

Action: Buying the newest gaming console

1st-order consequence: I spend two to three hours playing video games daily.

2nd-order consequence: I start to fall behind on my relationships, business, and personal hygiene.

3rd-order consequence: Life starts becoming more miserable.

4th-order consequence: I start giving video games more attention as a way to escape from reality.

5th-order consequence: My real-life problems become worse.

Why is it hard to predict future consequences when making that first decision? Simple: the answer is time.

Humans have a hard time wrapping their minds around time. I explained this in my first Instagram post on compound interest (also the first chapter of this book).

Instead of having time and second-order consequences working against you, make it work in your favor.

Always ask yourself, "Is this decision going to benefit me in the next three to five years?" If it's a yes, go for it. If it's a no, you probably shouldn't take that action.

It Is Expensive to Be Cheap, But Cheap to Be Expensive

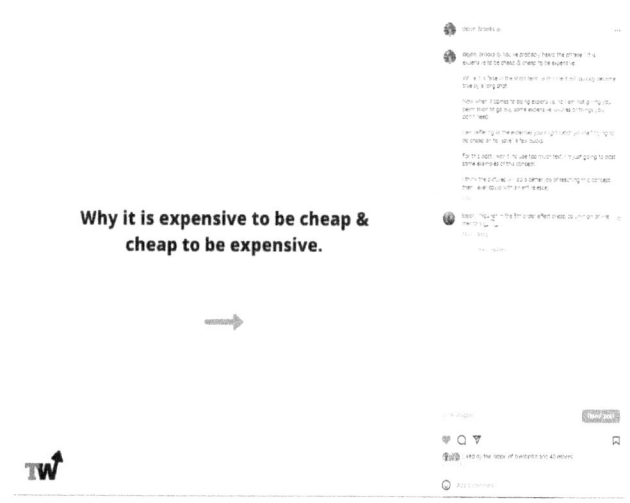

You've probably heard the phrase, "It is expensive to be cheap, but cheap to be expensive."

While it feels false in the short term, it will quickly become true with time.

When it comes to being expensive, I am not permitting you to buy expensive luxuries or things you don't need.

I am referring to the expenses you might catch yourself trying to be cheap with to "save" a few bucks.

For this chapter, I have little to say and instead will post some examples of this concept in the form of images I created in the past.

The pictures will better illustrate this concept.

Vehicle Maintenance

	Cheap	Expensive
1st Order Effect:	Don't fix the problem, fix it yourself cheaply	Spend a couple hundred to fix the issue
2nd Order Effect:	Another piece of the car that was in perfect condition now needs repair. Costs $750 To repair	Car is fixed & ready for the next 6 months.
3rd Order Effect:	Vehicle is undrivable. You have to pay $2500 to fix it all, buy another car or take uber/lyft	Your able to work on every opportunity.
4th Order Effect:	You spend $100 - $200 a week to uber to and back from work. You are late occasionally.	You gain a raise/promotion as you are met all unexpected expenses.
5th Order Effect:	Takes a loan to purchase another car.	You are able to save money & save up emergency fund.

Running Shoes

	Cheap	Expensive
1st Order Effect:	Save $25 to purchase the cheap brand	Spend an extra $25 for the high quality brand
2nd Order Effect:	Shoe breaks within 6 months of daily use	They provide maximum comfort, allowing you to run further/faster without pain
3rd Order Effect:	Spends another $125 to purchase the high quality brand	Due to the less pain, you are able to recover faster allowing you to train at higher levels
4th Order Effect:	Due to the cheap material on the cheap shoe, you must now go see a foot doctor. $500	Training longer/harder allows you to run at more advanced paces
5th Order Effect:	Doctor recommends some time off which will affect your health & training process.	At these levels, you are able to compete with others who are at the same level and faster than you.

Online Courses & Mentors

	Cheap	Expensive
1st Order Effect:	Watch free books & watch free videos	Spend $2,000 on a online course
2nd Order Effect:	You'll spend thousands of dollars on trial and error	Receive access to proven business's/sales models
3rd Order Effect:	You'll loose motivation & fall back to your original habits	Since you simplify & 10x, you will solve every problem you at ever break into
4th Order Effect:	You'll continue to waste time & money on things that don't matter	After your first few sales the rest will become easier.
5th Order Effect:	Your in the same spot financially 5 years later	You are now earning $10,000/month 1 year later.

Unprotected Sex

	Cheap	Expensive
1st Order Effect:	none ($0)	$3 for a pack of protection
2nd Order Effect:	Pregnancy	No kid
3rd Order Effect:	Spend thousands on preparing for a child	You are able to save & allocate funds to: kids investments, education & savings
4th Order Effect:	$10,000 baby delivery medical bill	Put your extra funds to invest financially
5th Order Effect:	Spend an average of $1500/month for food, insurance, diapers, toys, clothes etc.	You are now able to build the farm to comfortably raise a family without money being an issue

You can also view these images at presellyourstory.com/images

Comforting Lies vs. The Cold Hard Truth

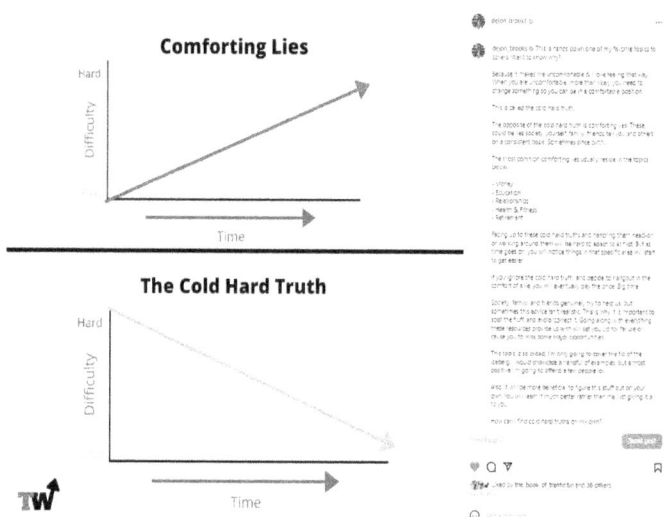

I love taking on the cold hard truth. Want to know why?

Because it makes me uncomfortable, and I love feeling that way. When you are uncomfortable, you likely need to change something to be in a comfortable position.

The opposite of the cold hard truth is comforting lies. These could be lies that society, yourself, your family, and friends tell you consistently. Sometimes since birth.

The most common comforting lies usually reside in the topics below.

- Money
- Education

- Relationships
- Health & Fitness
- Retirement

Facing up to these cold hard truths and handling them head-on or working around them will be hard to adapt to. But as time passes, you will notice things in that specific area will get easier.

If you ignore the cold hard truth and decide to hang out in the comfort of a lie, you will eventually pay the price. Big time.

Society, family, and friends genuinely try to help us, but sometimes their advice isn't realistic. This is why it is essential to spot the fluff and avoid it. Going along with everything these resources provide us with will set you up for failure or cause you to miss some significant opportunities.

How can I find cold hard truths on my own?

Simple: The cold hard truth is usually the most challenging option to handle upfront but gets easier over time.

As they say, if you do what's hard, your life will become easy. But if you do what's easy, your life will become hard.

Found something valuable in this chapter? Share it by taking a picture and tagging me on your Instagram stories @dejon_brooks!

Never Overstay Your Welcome

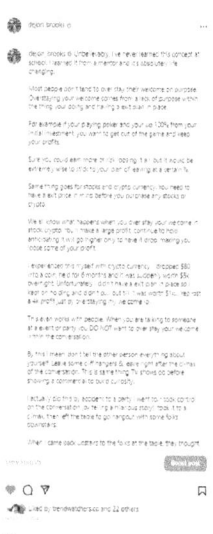

Never Overstay Your Welcome

I learned this concept from an online mentor, and it was hard to accept at first. But once I figured it out, it completely changed my life.

Most people don't overstay their welcome on purpose. Often, one of two things happens:

1) You're genuinely having a good time and want to stay longer.

2) You lack purpose within the thing you're doing and don't have an exit plan in place.

For example, if you're playing poker and are up 100% from your initial investment, it would be smart to get out of the game and keep your profits.

Sure, you could earn more but you could also risk losing it all. Even though it is hard, it is wise to stick to your original plan of leaving at a certain percentage.

The same thing goes for stocks and cryptocurrency. It would be best to have an exit price in mind before purchasing any stocks or crypto.

We all know what happens when you overstay your welcome in stock/crypto. You'll make a significant profit and continue to hold, anticipating it will go higher only to have it drop, causing you to lose your earnings.

I experienced this myself with cryptocurrency. I dropped $80 into a coin, held it for six months, and it was suddenly worth $5,500 overnight. Unfortunately, I didn't have an exit plan in place, so I kept holding and didn't pull out until it was worth $1k.

I lost 4k in extra earnings just by overstaying my welcome.

This concept works with people, too. When you are talking to someone at an event or party, you DO NOT want to overstay your welcome within the conversation.

By this, I mean don't tell the other person everything about yourself. Leave some cliffhangers and depart right after the climax of the conversation. This is the same thing TV shows do before showing a commercial to build curiosity.

I did this by accident at a party I went to mid 2020. I took control of the conversation (by telling a hilarious story), took it to a climax, and then left the table upstairs to hang out with some folks downstairs.

When I came back upstairs to the folks at the table, they thought I was the funniest person they'd ever met. They even wanted to exchange contacts as I was heading out.

To summarize this entire chapter, always have an exit plan in place, and when dealing with people at parties or networking events, always leave at the climax of the conversation/interaction.

You'll notice they will treat you differently when you see them again.

How Social Proof Works against You

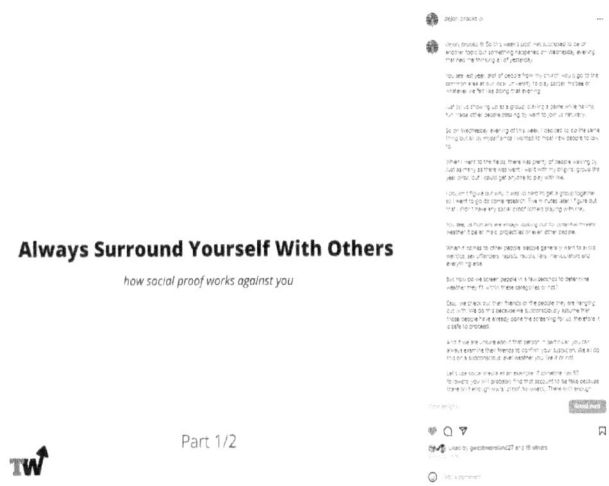

Always Surround Yourself With Others

how social proof works against you

Part 1/2

TW

This week's post was supposed to be on another topic, but something happened Wednesday evening that had me thinking all of yesterday.

You see, last year, many people from my church would go to the common area at our local university to play soccer, frisbee, or whatever we felt like doing that evening.

Just by us showing up as a group and playing a game while having fun, other people passing by want to join us naturally.

So Wednesday evening of this week, I decided to do the same thing but by myself since I wanted to meet new people to talk to.

When I went to the fields, plenty of people were walking by, but I couldn't get anyone to play with me.

I couldn't figure out why it was so hard to get a group together, so I went to do some research. Five minutes later, I realized I had no social proof (others playing with me).

You see, we humans are always looking out for potential threats. This can include animals, projectiles, or even other people.

How do we screen people in a few seconds to determine whether they are a danger or not?

Easy; we check out their friends and the people they hang out with. We do this because we subconsciously assume that those people have already done the screening for us; therefore, it is safe to proceed.

If you are unsure about a specific person, you can always examine their friends to confirm your suspicion. Whether you like it or not, we all do this subconsciously.

Let's use social media as an example. If someone has fifty followers, you may think that account is fake because there isn't enough social proof (followers). There aren't enough people telling you that this person is legit, so you assume a worst-case scenario (it's fake) and block/unfollow the account.

Even during talk shows and game shows. Why do you think they pay some people to be in the audience to make as much noise as possible? Social proof.

If they don't do this and just have an empty room, you may be interested in the show, but because the room is empty, you'll go watch something else.

I had this problem with my first software company. Most of my service took place in a central group chat, and I had no one there at the time. My service was so attractive and high quality that I could quickly sell spots within the group.

But, after my customers purchased and joined the group and saw they were the only ones there, they quickly requested a refund and left.

I then realized the importance of having beta testers in this group to provide valuable feedback and serve as social proof.

Back when I went to many networking events, I would always go by myself. It would always turn out okay. It was awkward at first, but I always was able to build some social momentum; I was able to make a handful of decent connections and end the night on a high note.

I once decided to bring a friend to one of these networking events. By having him serve as my social proof, I spoke with many people. Way more than usual. I even got my first mentor from this networking event.

That happened just by me having other people with me.

I recommend having others with you in social situations/environments such as events, parties, etc. Of course, there should be times when you should go solo and be alone, but sometimes, having others will make a difference. It's good to balance the two.

Usually, two or three people will do the trick, but you want to make sure the people you bring along won't drag you down, or the whole concept of bringing others with you will work against you.

No Is Discipline, Yes Is a Responsibility

No, Is Discipline

Yes, Is A Responsibility

TW

I was hiking Kennesaw Mountain with a friend the other day. He had to go to the restroom, so I waited outside. While waiting, I noticed someone had dropped their ID on the ground. When I saw it, I came up with the phrase, "Saying no is discipline, but yes is a responsibility."

I knew if I picked it up, I had to find a way to return it to the owner. I was committing myself to the task. Knowing the consequences, I picked it up, hoping the person who dropped it was nearby.

Unfortunately, she wasn't, so I planned on mailing it to her when I got home. When I got home, I realized we didn't have any stamps, so I had to personally deliver the ID to her house, which would take ninety minutes round trip.

The point of this story is that when you say "yes" to a task you are taking on, it could take a few extra hours/days/weeks to complete. For the task above, I thought it would take a few minutes to solve, BUT it took me over two hours to complete.

It would be nice to say yes to everyone, but we will overwhelm ourselves.

Because of this, it is okay to say no and pass on tasks sometimes.

When saying yes, you first need to ask yourself, *Does this task fit within my personal standards, finances, or life goals?*

In the example above, I accepted the task of returning that lady's ID because it fell within my personal standards.

I didn't have to think twice about it. I had to return it in case it got into the wrong hands.

Having personal goals and standards in place makes decision-making extremely easy. All you have to do is glance at a situation you are presented with, and within seconds, you will know what to do.

Now, understand that when you say yes, you must execute and finish that task 100%. There are no maybes; either you do it or you don't.

I've been applying this concept for an entire year, and not only does it allow you to have more time to yourself, but it also helps improve your mental health.

Remember, no is discipline, and yes is a responsibility.

The Victim Card

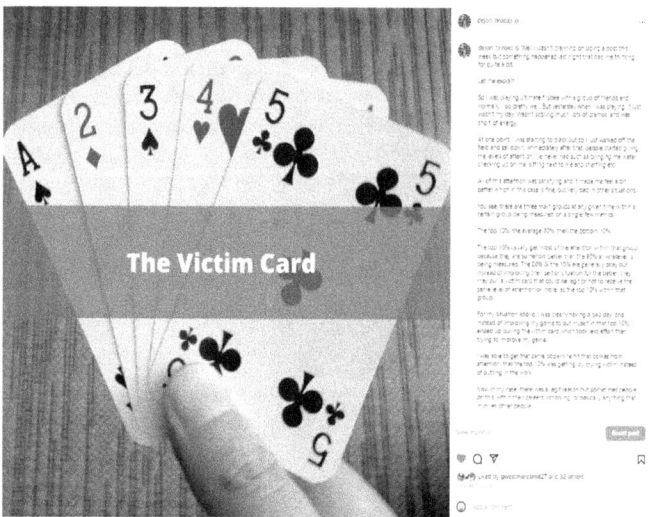

I was playing ultimate frisbee with a group of friends, and I usually do pretty good, but I wasn't doing well on this particular day. I was scoring little, had many cramps, and lacked energy.

I started blacking out at one point, so I walked off the field and sat down. Immediately after that, people started giving me levels of attention I've never had, such as bringing me water, checking up on me, sitting next to me, chatting, etc.

All of this attention was satisfying, and it made me feel a bit better, which in this case is fine but very bad in other situations.

You see, there are three main groups at any given time within a specific group being measured on a single/few metrics.

The top 10%, the average 80%, then the bottom 10%.

The top 10% usually get most of the attention within that group because they are better than the 90% at whatever is being measured. The 80% and the 10% are generally okay, but they may pull a victim card instead of improving themselves. Pulling the victim card allows you to get the same level of attention (or more) as the top 10% within that group.

In my situation above, I was having a bad day, and instead of improving my game to put myself in that top 10%, I pulled the victim card, which took less effort than trying to improve my game.

I got the same dopamine hit that the top 10% was getting by crying victim instead of doing the work.

There was a legitimate reason in my case, but sometimes people do this purposely within their careers, schooling, or anything involving other people.

Sometimes, these claims are legit, but don't let them hold you back from improving yourself.

Some people are so trapped within this cycle that there is no incentive to improve their situation.

Motive vs. Morality

Motive VS Morality

I believe that everyone is nice and friendly.

You will also understand this if you look past people's immediate actions and understand their motives first.

For example, you're on the highway, and someone cuts you off. Is this person mean?

In your eyes, yes, but what if I told you their exit was coming up soon and they were fifteen minutes late for work?

That could change your perspective on things.

What if someone tackled an innocent bystander who was running? This is clearly out of the norm, but what if I told you that the person running committed another crime and the bystander who tackled him witnessed it?

In most cases, the motives are somewhat legit and are sometimes unavoidable. But unfortunately, some people make the wrong choices to satisfy their reason.

For example, a mother's children may be starving, so she steals.

This is why, before I judge anyone, I do my best to understand their motive first. Understanding people's motives will save time, money, relationships, etc.

As I grew Trend Watchers, a few people requested refunds for my service immediately after purchasing. I don't mind refunding, but these people would buy to view all of our data, save it, and then request a refund. Instead of calling them leechers and disputing their refunds, I looked into their motive.

Once I understood their motive, I adjusted my product to prevent the problem from happening again.

Remember that everyone has a motive.

How You Do One Thing Is How You Do Everything

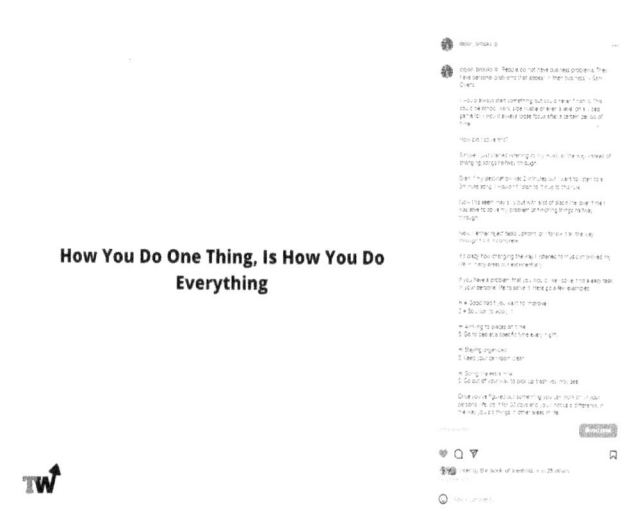

How You Do One Thing, Is How You Do Everything

TW

"People do not have business problems. They have personal problems that appear in their business."

– Sam Ovens

Growing up, I always struggled with finishing things I would start. This affected me with school, side hustles, or even a level on a video game. I would always lose focus after a certain period.

How did I solve this?

Simple: I just started listening to my music in its entirety instead of changing songs halfway through.

Even if my destination was two minutes away, but I wanted to listen to a three-minute song, I wouldn't listen to it due to this rule.

Now, this seems silly, but with a lot of discipline, I solved my problem of finishing things halfway through over time.

Now, I either reject tasks upfront or follow through until they're complete.

It's wild; changing how I listened to music improved my life in many areas.

If you have a problem that you would like to solve or would like to acquire a new habit, you should first find an easy task in your personal life to solve it.

Here are a few examples:

Habit: Arriving at places on time
Solution: Go to bed at a specific time every night

Habit: Staying organized
Solution: Keep your car/room clean

Habit: Going the extra mile
Solution: Go out of your way to pick up trash you may see

Once you've figured out something you can work on in your personal life, do it for thirty days, and you'll notice a difference in how you do things in other areas.

Success Leaves Clues

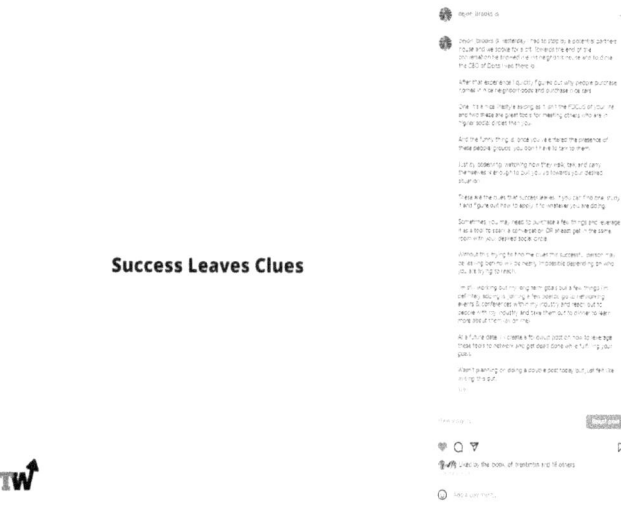

Success Leaves Clues

I recently stopped by a friend's house, and we spoke briefly. Towards the end of the conversation, he showed me his neighbor's house and told me the CEO of Delta lived there.

After that experience, I quickly figured out why people purchased homes in nice neighborhoods and bought expensive cars.

One, it's a nice lifestyle. Two, these are great tools for meeting other high-level people.

And the funny thing is, once you've entered the presence of these people/groups, you don't have to talk to them.

Observing and watching how they walk, talk, and carry themselves is enough to pull you up.

These are the clues that success leaves. If you can find one, study it and figure out how to apply it to whatever you are doing.

Sometimes, you may need to purchase a few things and leverage them as a tool to spark a conversation—*or* at least get in the same room with your desired social circle.

This is necessary to find the clues this successful person may be leaving behind, depending on who you are trying to reach.

Found something valuable in this chapter? Share it by taking a picture and tagging me on your Instagram stories @dejon_brooks!

Always Plan for Worst-Case Scenarios

I was getting ready to go somewhere this morning and noticed I only had about ninety miles left in my gas tank.

My destination was about thirty-five miles away, and my gas light usually goes off around sixty miles. According to my calculations, I can reach my destination without turning on my gas light.

I thought about it briefly and planned for a worst-case scenario by filling up my tank.

Doing this allowed me to focus on other important issues during that drive.

Had I done it later, I would have been focusing on my gas bar the entire drive *while* looking for gas stations to stop at. I would have wasted so much mental energy on a little task.

I do not do any of the work for the company I run. I'm more of the thinker behind the strategy/creativity.

To get unique ideas daily, I have to try my best to live stress-free, and the best way to do that is to plan for the worst-case scenario.

Planning for a worst-case scenario gives you a birds-eye view of any situation. And the best part is, it doesn't get any worse. Either it works, or you default to your worst-case scenario.

Here are a few areas that I apply this to:

- Finances
- Meeting people
- Projects
- Clothing (rain or shine)
- Oversleeping

Planning for worst-case scenarios will also decrease the chances of executing that plan because you can focus on your end goal without worrying about wasting energy on the uncertainty of failure.

Life Lessons from Pokemon

Life Lessons From Pokémon

I've decided to change things up for November, 2020 by playing a Pokemon game from scratch.

It's been a good three or four years since I've last touched a Pokemon game, and surprisingly, I've learned a few things from it.

Even if you don't play games, I still recommend reading this chapter.

1) Talk to everyone

To break my fear of walking in front of a Pokemon trainer who wants to battle, I just spoke to everyone, whether they were a trainer who tried to fight or not.

Talking to people who were not part of the main storyline allowed me to get tons of cool free items, tips, and wisdom that I would have never received had I not asked.

The same thing can be applied to life. You can discover opportunities or get small wins by just showing up and talking.

2) Always improvise

So whenever my main Pokemon was down, I had to rely on the rest of my team, which was dramatically weaker. I had to use potions, full heals, and pure luck to overcome any unexpected battles on my way to the Poké Center (the place to heal your team).

Understand that your original plans will never work out, so be prepared to do a lot of improvising!

3) Always improve yourself

So when I started, I told myself I would challenge every Pokemon trainer I saw to a battle.

By doing this, my main Pokemon became incredibly stronger than the Pokemon in the main storyline, making the game a breeze to plow through. (I'm twenty levels higher than what I'm supposed to be without any trading.)

If you do what is hard today, tomorrow will be easy.

4) The best defense is offense

There is a move called "Protect." It protects you from all damage for that round.

I think the move is useless because when the next turn comes, you're still in the same position. Literally, nothing has changed.

It would have been more efficient to go offensive and end the round quicker than to stall it for later.

To translate this lesson into reality, why stall tasks for tomorrow when you can clear them today?

5) Always save the game

Or, in other words, always document everything. It's insurance that will save you big time.

If you have some free time, play a video game. You'll learn a few incredible lessons from them.

Creating Your Own Luck

Creating Your Own Luck

Part 1: Showing Up

A few days ago, I had the best Pokemon battle ever. Going into the match, I knew I would lose due to a few moves left across my Pokemon.

I wasn't going to try but decided to give it a shot, and guess what?

I won!

It's difficult to explain it in writing, but a series of consecutive events occurred, and the chances of all these events happening were around 1/10,000.

Fortunately, these odds were in my favor, resulting in my win.

The same thing can be said about life. Hard work won't save you. It is going to come down to luck.

Fortunately, you can create your own luck by constantly put yourself in places that will help you succeed.

When I was running my social media marketing agency back in high school, I would attend a bunch of networking events. Eventually, I attended one and found a good mentor that set me off in the right direction.

Even with Trend Watchers, I would post the website link on various directories, marketplaces, and forums. This helped me get a lot of users, press, attention, and proof of concept.

School teaches you the formula for working hard, but in reality, it's a combination of hard, focused work and some luck.

Found something valuable in this chapter? Share it by taking a picture and tagging me on your Instagram stories @dejon_brooks!

Failure Is Temporary, Regret Is Forever

I've been eyeing a unique opportunity to take action on for the past year.

What stopped me? Fear of rejection.

It wasn't until recently that I noticed someone else had taken action on this opportunity I spotted and succeeded.

Immediately, I started telling myself subconsciously that this could have been me, and now this scenario will haunt me for the rest of my life.

That's one of the worst things about regret. Once the opportunity has passed, you will never stop asking yourself what would have happened if you did it.

You will always wonder how much better or worse your life would be had you succeeded at the task you were assessing.

On the other hand, failure is a win/win scenario in this case. If luck isn't on your side, you will gain wisdom that will always push you in the correct direction.

I remember when I asked my first crush for her number in high school. It was super awkward, and I cringe at it to this day, but from that failure:

1) I was able to get a great story out of it.

2) It taught me how to improve my next approach.

In this case, failure worked in my favor. Also, in high school, I had the opportunity to invest in cryptocurrency during the 2017–2018 bull run.

I originally wanted to throw in $4,500–$5,000, but my parents didn't let me. They saw the move as "risky" and would only let me put in $100 ($80 after fees).

Fast-forward a few months, that $80 grew to around $5,500.

I would have had over $300,000 before I had unstuck to my original plan of putting in $4,500.

The regret of not putting in that original amount still gets me to this day. Even though I learned a lot from the experience, the thought of how my life would be different if I had taken the risk will haunt me until I die.

One of the things I do to help me avoid not taking action on opportunities is to listen to the song "It's My Life" by Bon Jovi frequently.

Read the lyrics if you can; they're very motivating.

Anyway, never forget failure is temporary, but regret is forever.

You Must Be Selfish If You Want to Achieve Anything

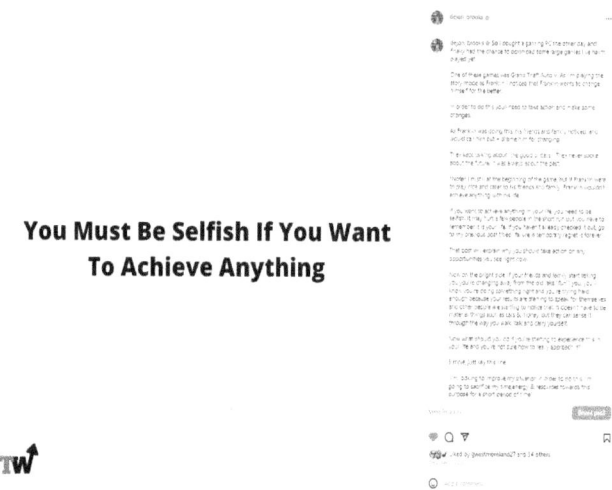

I bought a gaming PC the other day and finally had the chance to download some big games I haven't played yet.

One of these games was *Grand Theft Auto V*. As I was playing the story mode as Franklin, I noticed that Franklin wanted to change himself for the better.

As Franklin did this, his friends and family noticed and would call him out and shame him for changing.

They kept talking about "the good old days." They never spoke about the future. It was always about the past.

I'm still at the beginning of the game, but if Franklin were to play nice and cater to his friends and family, Franklin wouldn't achieve anything with his life. He had to adjust social circles to change his life circumstances.

If you want to achieve anything, you need to be selfish. It may hurt a few people in the short run, but this is your life.

On the bright side, if your friends and family tell you you're changing away from the old (aka "fun") you, you'll know you're doing something right. You're trying hard enough, and because your results are starting to speak for themselves, other people are noticing. It doesn't have to be material things such as cars and money, but they can sense it through how you walk, talk, and carry yourself.

What should you do if you're starting to experience this?

One of my favorite lines to tell people is, "I'm looking to improve my situation, and to do this, I'm going to sacrifice my time, energy, and resources towards this purpose for a short period."

If you keep getting resistance, repeat the line but rephrase it differently. If you want to change your life, you need to be selfish for a bit.

Found something valuable in this chapter? Share it by taking a picture and tagging me on your Instagram stories @dejon_brooks!

Disproportionate Inputs & Outputs

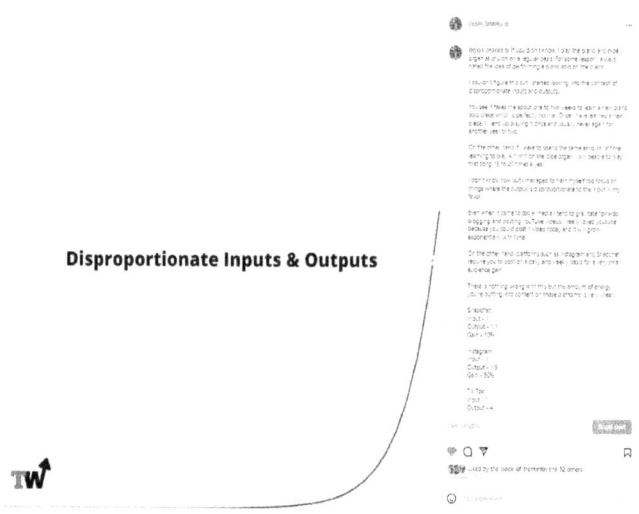

I play the piano and pipe organ at church regularly. For some reason, I always hated performing a piano solo.

I couldn't figure why, until I came across the concept of disproportionate inputs and outputs.

It took me nearly two weeks to learn a new piano solo, which is perfectly normal. Once I have learned a new piece, I'll play it once in church and never again for another year or two.

On the other hand, if I spent the same amount of time learning a hymn on the pipe organ, I would be able to play that song fifteen to twenty times a year.

Once I realized this, it made more sense why I preferred the organ over the piano. I got more out of learning a piece on the organ than the piano.

Even on social media, I gravitate towards blogging and posting YouTube videos. I loved YouTube because you could post one video today, and it will grow exponentially with time.

On the other hand, platforms such as Instagram and Snapchat require you to post daily and weekly for a small audience gain.

Nothing is wrong with this, but the amount of energy you put into content on those platforms is linear.

Snapchat

Input – 1

Output – 1.1

Gain – 10%

Instagram

Input – 1

Output – 1.5

Gain – 50%

TikTok

Input – 1

Output – 4

Gain – 400%

YouTube

Input – 1

Output – 10

Gain – 1,000%

These numbers vary between creators, but these are my numbers from the experiments I have run on my platforms.

After discovering this, I spend most of my time creating YouTube videos and blog posts due to the high input-to-output differences. This has allowed me to grow my brands exponentially while putting in the least effort.

Disproportionate inputs and outputs not only exist online. This concept can also be applied to your personal life. Ask yourself, *What bad/good habits can I drop/gain that will give me a disproportionate output in the positives?*

Doing a few of these will change your quality of life exponentially.

Systems vs. Tactics

Systems

- Systems are flows that turn a decent output/profit consistently

Tactics

- Tactics are strategies designed to magnify specific functions of the system

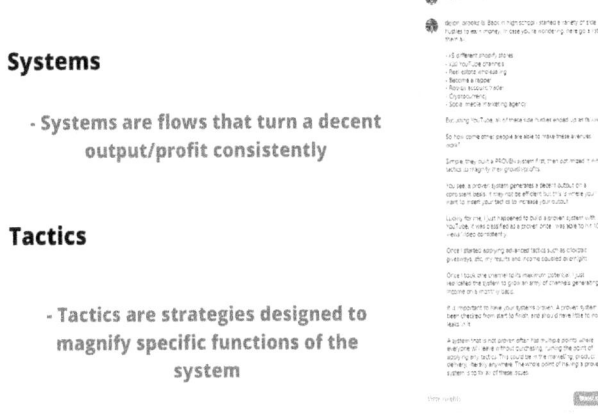

Back in high school, I started a variety of side hustles to earn money. Here is a list of them all:

- x5 different Shopify stores
- x20 YouTube channels
- Real estate wholesaling
- Become a rapper
- Roblox account trader
- Cryptocurrency
- Social media marketing agency

Excluding YouTube, all of these side hustles ended up as failures.

How come other people can make these moneymaking methods work?

They built a PROVEN system first, then optimized it with tactics to magnify their growth and profits.

You see, a proven system generates a decent output consistently. It may need to be more efficient, but this is where you'll want to insert your tactics to increase your output.

Luckily, I built a proven system with YouTube. It was classified as proven once I hit 100k views/video consistently.

Once I started applying advanced tactics such as clickbait, trends, and giveaways, my results and income doubled overnight.

Once I took one channel to its maximum potential, I replicated the system to grow an army of channels.

It is essential to have your systems proven. A proven system has been checked from start to finish and should have little to no leaks.

A system that is not proven often has multiple points where everyone will leave without purchasing, ruining the point of applying any tactics. This could be in marketing, product delivery, or anywhere else. The whole point of having a proven system is to fix all of these issues.

If you do not have a proven system, continue learning about different skills across various subjects. Here is a list I threw together for you!

- Marketing
- Sales
- Productivity

- Paid/organic traffic sources

- Relationship management

- Web design

- Legal stuff & Accounting

Once you have learned a handful of tactics/skills, you could deploy them on proven systems you might come across or create in the future.

Why do people buy businesses?

Answer: Because established businesses are often already a proven systems. All you need to do is apply key tactics in certain areas to increase the revenue exponentially.

Sometimes, It Pays off Being Stupid

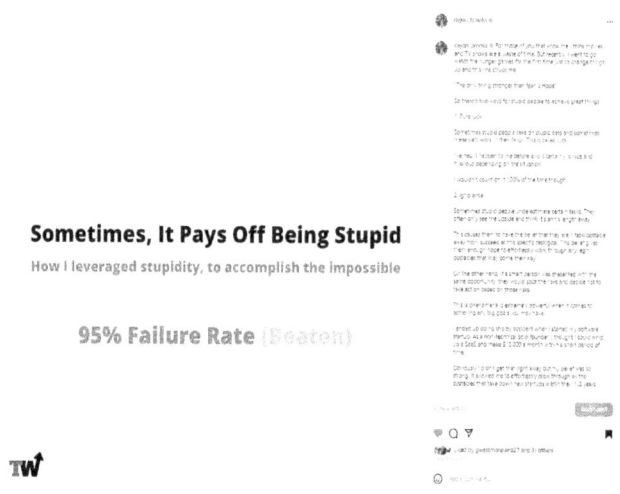

For those who know me, I think movies and TV shows are a waste of time. But recently, I went to watch *The Hunger Games* for the first time to change things up, and this line struck me: "The only thing stronger than fear is hope."

There are two ways for stupid people to achieve great things:

1. Pure luck

Sometimes, stupid people take on stupid bets, and sometimes, these bets work in their favor. This is called luck.

I've had it happen to me before, and it certainly is nice and hilarious, depending on the situation.

I wouldn't count on it 100% of the time, though.

2. Ignorance

Sometimes, stupid people underestimate specific tasks. They often only see the upside and think it's an arm's length away.

This causes them to believe that they are one task/obstacle away from succeeding at this specific task/goal. This belief gives them enough hope to work through any challenges that may come their way effortlessly.

On the other hand, if an intelligent person were presented with the same opportunity, they would spot the risks and decide not to take action based on those risks.

This phenomenon is compelling when it comes to achieving any big goals you may have.

I ended up doing this by accident when I started my software start-up Trend Watchers. As a nontechnical solo founder, I thought I could whip up a SaaS and make $10,000 a month quickly.

Unfortunately the opposite happened, but my belief was so strong it allowed me to effortlessly plow through all the obstacles that take down new start-ups within their first year or two.

I am not stupid; I just didn't know much about the software start-up space. Due to my ignorance, this allowed me to succeed and make it to the growth phase of my SaaS.

Had I taken the logical route, I would have determined that there was no way I could raise $250k in venture capital and hire employees as a 19-year-old with no start-up experience.

This is how stupid people win.

You NEED Luck to Get Opportunities

Fun fact: I have a digital journal I've been writing in for the past five years with over 300,000 words (600 pages!).

We've all heard that you must tell people a story to keep them interested or get them to buy from you. This sounds easy on paper, but in reality, it is challenging and tricky to apply if you don't know what you're doing.

When starting Trend Watchers, I had a very limited marketing budget. I had to rely on organic marketing and word of mouth.

One tactic I implemented to improve my conversion rate was to tell my story to every user who signed up on the platform.

Even though I increased my conversions by emailing every user who signed up, something else happened. I started getting more opportunities coming my way. Here is a list of what I came across:

- Press opportunities
- Networking with big names
- Partnerships
- Valuable user feedback, which was used to release critical updates

Had I not told my story and included a picture of myself in that email, 90% of the opportunities that came my way would have gone elsewhere.

In life, you need luck.

Opportunities and solutions will not fall from the sky into your hands. You'll have to get out of the house, open up your phone or email, and put yourself out there to increase the odds of getting lucky.

One of my favorite and most reliable ways to get lucky consistently is to tell everyone I meet my story when appropriate.

Telling people your story is an easy way to stand out from the competition, make an emotional connection, and eventually inspiring people to take action.

If you need help finding new opportunities, I challenge you to write and tell an exciting story about yourself and share it when appropriate.

You will be amazed as to what opportunities will present themselves to you.

The Importance of Switching Things Up

Yep, that's a loaf of bread I'm holding.

It's gluten-free. I usually eat wheat but decided to switch things up temporarily. I'm also showing my face for the first time over Instagram.

Why?

You see, it is important to switch things up now and then. We are creatures of habit. Doing a task a certain way over a period of time will naturally become a habit.

This is good initially but bad in the long run because your brain isn't experiencing anything new.

Even when I'm driving back from an destination, I do my best to take a completely different route, even if it is entirely out of my way.

The cool thing about switching things up occasionally is that it exposes you to different perspectives.

For example, if you've always lived in your hometown, you should change things by moving out of your state or country.

It may be difficult to adjust at first, but change always leads us to growth and gives us a new perspective in life.

This new perspective gives us experience, which can make you become a more interesting person to speak to.

Anyway, I'm about to make some sandwiches. I'm hungry.

Remember to change things up, though!

Wearing the Same Outfit Every Day (90-Day Report)

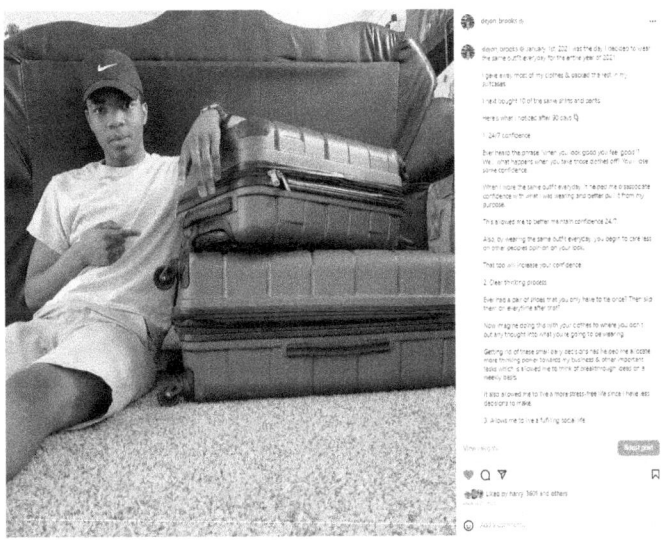

January 1st, 2021, was the day I decided to wear the same outfit every day for 2021. I gave away most of my clothes and packed the rest in my suitcases. I then bought ten of the same shirts and pants.

Here's what I noticed after 90 days:

1. 24/7 confidence

Ever heard the phrase "When you look good, you feel good"? Well, what happens when you take those clothes off? You'll lose some confidence.

Wearing the same outfit daily helped me disassociate confidence from what I was wearing and get it from my purpose instead.

This allowed me to maintain confidence 24/7 better.

Also, by wearing the same outfit daily, you begin to care less about other people's opinions of your look.

That, too, will increase your confidence.

2. Clear thinking process

Have you ever had a pair of shoes that you only had to tie once? Then slip them on every time after that?

Now imagine doing this with your clothes so that you don't think about what you'll be wearing.

Getting rid of these small daily decisions has helped me allocate more thinking power toward my business and other essential tasks, allowing me to think of breakthrough ideas weekly.

It also allowed me to live a more stress-free life since I had fewer decisions.

3. It allows me to live a fulfilling social life

Ever had a nice outfit and been self-conscious of it the entire time you were out with friends?

Because I was wearing an outfit that could be easily replaced, I could focus on enjoying myself instead of thinking about ruining a pair of clothes or wondering if people liked my outfit.

In the past, I missed out on amazing experiences because I didn't want to get my shoes or clothes messed up.

It's wild how a pair of clothes can hold us back from enjoying ourselves trying to impress others who aren't even paying attention.

Reaching Perfection

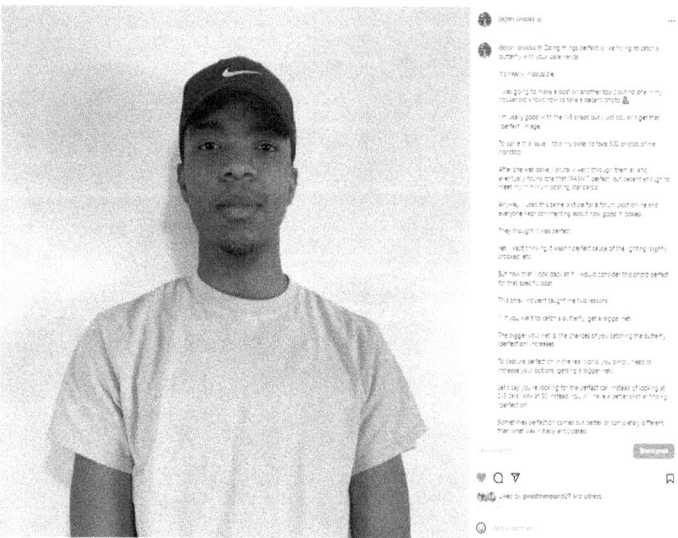

Trying to do things perfectly is like catching a butterfly with your bare hands. It's nearly impossible.

I was going to make a post on another topic, but no one in my household knows how to take a decent photo.

I'm usually good with 1–5 spontaneous snaps, but I couldn't get that "perfect" image. To solve this issue, I told my sister to take 100 photos of me nonstop.

After she was done, I brutally went through them all and eventually found one that could have been better but decent enough to meet my minimum posting standards.

Anyway, I used this same picture for a forum post online, and everyone kept commenting about how good it looked. They thought it was perfect.

Yet, I kept thinking it wasn't good. Now that I look back at it, this photo is perfect for that specific post.

This minor incident taught me two lessons:

1. Get a bigger net if you want to catch a butterfly

The bigger your net is, the chances of you catching the butterfly (perfection) increases.

To capture perfection in the real world, you must increase your options (getting a bigger net).

Let's say you're looking for the perfect car. Instead of looking at two or three cars, look at thirty instead. You will have a better shot at finding "perfection."

Sometimes, perfection comes out better or completely different than what was initially anticipated.

2. Others rarely notice your mistakes/flaws

I play the piano and organ at my church on Sundays. Occasionally, I'll make a minor mistake here and there. When I make a mistake, I think everybody also notices that mistake.

To cover these mistakes, I improvise or simply get back on track without stopping my flow.

By doing this, hardly anyone notices my mistakes unless they are really into the music.

The PROCESS of improvising is another form of perfection. We only realize this after the event has passed.

The best way to achieve perfection is to take action now, increase options, *or* improvise if resources and time are limited.

Always Pick Up the Change on the Ground

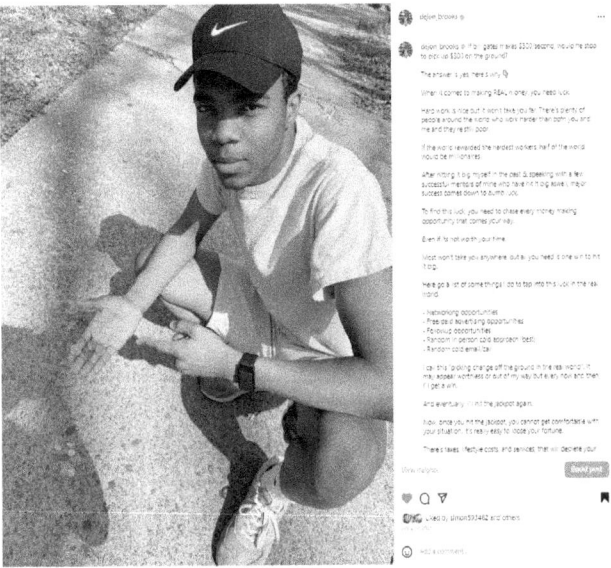

If Bill Gates makes $300 a second, would he stop to pick up $300 on the ground?

If you were to ask me, the answer is yes. Here's why.

When it comes to making REAL money, you need luck.

Hard work is excellent, but it won't take you far. There are plenty of people around the world who work harder than both you and me, and they're still poor.

If the world rewarded the hardest workers, half of the world would be millionaires. After hitting it big myself in the past and speaking with a few successful mentors who have also hit it big, major success comes down to dumb luck.

To find this luck, you need to chase every moneymaking opportunity that comes your way.

Even if it's not worth your time right now.

Most will take you nowhere, but all you need is one win to hit it big.

Here is a list of things I do to tap into this luck in the real world:

- Networking opportunities
- Free/paid advertising opportunities
- Follow-up opportunities
- Random in-person cold approach (best)
- Random cold email/call

I call this "picking change off the ground in the real world." It may appear worthless or out of my way, but I'll get a win every now and then.

And eventually, I'll hit the jackpot again.

Once you hit the jackpot, you cannot get comfortable with your situation. It's really easy to lose your fortune.

There are taxes, lifestyle costs, and services that will deplete your stash fast. Also, you'll never know how long the money will continue rolling in from your most recent jackpot.

It can slow down a few years from now, which is why you should always pick the change off the ground to find more opportunities.

This will keep your streak rolling.

Once luck goes away, you'll never know how long it will take to hit the jackpot again. Sometimes, never, but remember, no matter how good your situation is, always pick up the change off the ground.

Good times turn into bad times, and bad times turn into good times.

Found something valuable in this chapter? Share it by taking a picture and tagging me on your Instagram stories @dejon_brooks!

My Accountability Partner

This is my accountability partner, Riley Cardwell. We met almost a year ago (at the time of this Instagram post), and I finally got to meet him in person yesterday.

How did we meet?

Over a year ago, I purchased a $2,000 course from Sam Ovens. This was one of the best decisions I've made after high school.

A few months into the program, a new feature was released where you can partner with other students and become each other's accountability partners.

So, I signed up and waited a few days for my potential matches to return. When my results came back, I had three people to choose from, and the second I saw Riley's profile, I knew he was the one.

Why Riley?

Well, we were around the same age and in similar niches, so I knew it would be a good match. All my other options were okay, but they were much older and in different time zones.

After I chose Riley, I introduced myself through email, and days later, we hopped on our first call over Discord.

Our first call was all over the place. We didn't know how to structure the call, there were technical difficulties, etc. But after our first few calls, we got the hang of it.

Having an accountability partner has been so helpful and refreshing. It's nice being able to go to someone to exchange ideas, get a second opinion, and hold me accountable to my goals.

It also taught me the importance of setting aside my issues/concerns and listening to the other person. Listening to the other person and helping them solve their problems has helped me figure out how to solve my problems.

Riley also taught me a lot of cool things I would have never thought of trying on my own…

To name a few:

- Sleep-tracking bands
- Cold, consistent email outreach with software

- Reading physical books again

- Lots of dating/self-development advice

- Notion

But I'm grateful to have you as an accountability partner, and I can't wait to see where both of us will be a few years from now.

Bad Luck Will Turn into Good Luck

It's been a while since I've been camping, so I decided to join a group to doing Blood Mountain (located in Georgia).

Everything went well. We did the hike, found good spots to set up camp, and made a friend along the way. But there was one problem.

I forgot my sleeping bag.

I had a few extra jackets I could wear, but that wasn't enough to retain my heat. So I was shivering all night.

Because of this, I couldn't sleep *at all* and pulled an all-nighter. While I patiently waited for the sunrise the entire night, there was nothing I could do. I had:

- No cell service
- It was too cold to write
- I couldn't walk back to the cars
- My feet and hands were numb
- Couldn't borrow gear

I was helpless, and there was nothing I could do. I just had to suck it up for the remainder of the night and count the minutes passing by. Luckily, I knew I had a few hours to suffer then everything would be alright.

So what did I do? I waited, and my bad fortune turned into good fortune within a few hours.

In life, we will experience all sorts of pains and trials. These pains can include:

- Breakup
- Death
- Finances
- Uncertainty

These things might suck at the moment, but as you put some time behind it and keep your head up, your bad luck WILL turn into good luck. Not might, but WILL.

The question is, how long are you willing to push forward without giving up? Bad luck will eventually turn into good luck. And good luck will eventually turn into bad luck.

This process could take a few hours, days, or even years. But the tides WILL turn to the opposite side eventually.

Why is it important to know this concept?

Well, if you are experiencing a lot of "bad luck," you can leverage this theory as hope to know that good times are around the corner. This will give you the strength to endure whatever you may be going through.

If life is treating you very well, you must humble yourself and prepare for when times become challenging. No matter how well you have it, your good fortune will turn into bad fortune.

Found something valuable in this chapter? Share it by taking a picture and tagging me on your Instagram stories @dejon_brooks!

Achieving Happiness

A few years ago, there was a period where I felt utterly lonely and felt like throwing in the towel. I was homeschooled, had no real friends, and life sucked. Exactly one year later, I was helping thousands of people around my age battle depression, suicidal thoughts, etc.

So many people were reaching out to me; I couldn't handle them all. This was one of the most fulfilling periods of my life. There was also a period when I was flat-broke and owned no assets.

Fast-forward a few months, and I was able to build a machine that completely changed that.

Within the photo displayed at the beginning of this chapter lies objects that resemble happiness, sadness, success, failure, and joy from projects I've taken on in the past.

From putting up signs in the rain, skipping school to attend networking events, encountering bears, writing proposals at 3 in the morning, and sending out thousands of cold emails/calls, I would never trade my experiences for anything else.

Life is about managing and leveraging your downside to turn yourself into a new character. This new character will enable you to reach new heights your old character couldn't.

Even though today may suck, know that it'll all be worth it as long as you keep moving forward. Whatever you do, do not give up! It is better to fail than not do anything at all. Failure will hurt for a bit, but you'll laugh it off a few weeks later.

Regret will eat you alive 'til the day you die because you'll never know the outcome and how that could have changed your life. But appreciate the struggle and write your experiences in a journal—especially on your worst days. In the future, you'll look back and realize the pursuit of overcoming the struggle will be one of the happiest periods of your life.

The measure of a fulfilling life isn't the amount of successes one has. It is by measuring the difference between your worst and best days. The bigger the gap, the more fulfilling it becomes.

Set Your Goal as the Standard

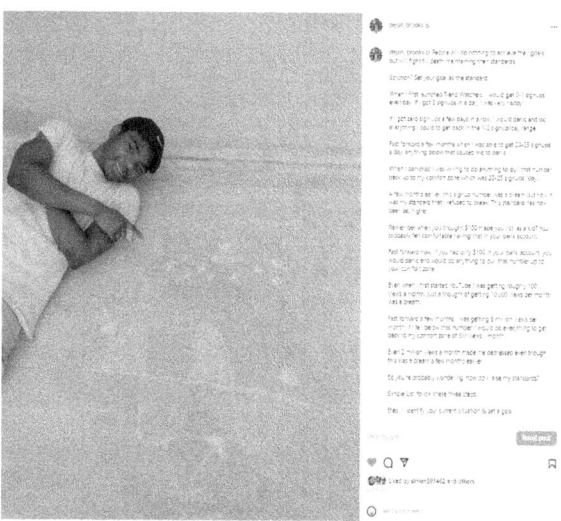

People will do nothing to achieve their goals but will fight to maintain their standards.

Solution? Set your goal as the standard.

When I first launched Trend Watchers, I got 0–1 sign-ups daily. If I got three sign-ups in a day, I was delighted. If I got zero sign-ups a few days in a row, I would panic and do everything I could to get back in the 1–2 sign-up/day range.

Fast-forward a few months, I increased this number to 20–25 daily sign-ups. Anything below that would cause me to panic. When I panicked, I was willing to do anything to regain that number to my comfort zone of 20–25 sign-ups/day.

A few months earlier, this sign-up number was a dream, but now it was my standard that I refused to break. Remember when you thought $100 made you rich as a kid? You probably felt comfortable having that in your bank account.

If you had only $100 in your bank account, you would panic and do anything to raise that number up to your comfort zone. Even when I first started YouTube, I got roughly 100 views monthly. Just the thought of getting 10,000 views per month was a dream.

Fast-forward a few months, and I was getting three million views per month. If I fell below that number, I would do everything to return to my three-million-views-per-month comfort zone.

Even two million views a month made me depressed, even though this was a dream a few months earlier.

How can you raise your standards? Just follow these three steps:

Step 1: Identify your current situation and set a goal

This step aims to identify your panic zone, comfort zone, and dream.

Step 2: Shoot as high as you can toward your goal

Even if your goal is unrealistic, shoot as high as you can. You'll be surprised at how far you'll get.

Step 3: Hold the peak and set it as the new standard

Once you feel like you can't go any higher, do your best to hold that position for as long as possible.

This will establish your new comfort zone. I've been using this tactic for the past few years to reach higher highs, and it works every single time.

Found something valuable in this chapter? Share it by taking a picture and tagging me on your Instagram stories @dejon_brooks!

How to Turn Any Situation into a Win/Win

Recently, I was forced to attend a three-hour presentation. Before it started, I knew what was up and figured it was a sales pitch. Instead of complaining about how it would be a waste of time, I decided to make myself a winner by looking for tactics I could apply to my business.

By the time the presentation was over, I had a long list of ideas to apply to my business. Some of these ideas made me more money.

I was able to do this because I had a winner's mindset. No matter how bad your situation may be, it would be best if you always looked for ways to turn that scenerio into a win/win.

When I had my first breakup a few years ago, I didn't sit around helplessly complaining about my situation. Instead, I decided to turn this breakup into a story. I used the story for one of the Facebook ads I ran, and it worked like a charm. I also used this breakup story as a hook to get people's attention so that they could listen to the rest of my pitch.

In 2017, I got around three million views a month on YouTube. Around the same time, my channel got demonetized, and my income quickly shattered.

Instead of complaining about this, I turned myself into a winner by starting multiple online businesses that replaced my income. I bought into a program for around $12,500 a few months ago. After hanging in the group for a few days, I realized the quality of the service could have been better.

Instead of complaining and asking for a refund, I decided to turn myself into a winner. This company had a killer sales process, so I installed the same process for Trend Watchers. After doing that, I quickly gained back my $12,500 and became a winner.

There are three ways you can make yourself a winner in any situation:

1. Turn it into a story and leverage it
2. Look for ideas and tactics you can apply in your personal/business life
3. Observe and learn from others' mistakes

Complaining is easy to do, but it barely benefits you. If you're going to suffer, at least find a way to benefit from it.

Chaos vs. Stasis

Many people go through life existing instead of living, and earlier this year, I caught myself existing. Here's how I changed that.

Last week, a group of friends and I went to a large outdoor party. There was karaoke, and I'd never done it before. Everyone was hesitant to go up and sing, so I did it for the first time.

I actually ended up enjoying it. I was able to live out my dream of becoming a "rock star" with a live audience.

After moving to Provo, Utah, I made the goal to meet two new people every day. To make it challenging:

- I had to collect their name
- I had to speak with them for at least two minutes

- I couldn't count the same person twice

This forced me to set my schedule to where I was outside the house at a different spot every day. Maintaining this goal allowed me to meet many amazing people with unique backgrounds, stories, and interests.

Meeting all these people and having meaningful conversations with them allowed me to feel like I was living life. Along with this, I've been:

- Going on random road trips
- Trying new foods
- Reading cool books
- Listening to podcasts
- Not letting fear prevent me from trying something

One of the best ways to start living life is to introduce chaos within in. Living a static and repetitive life makes the days blend depressingly. If you feel like you are living a stagnant life, look for ways to introduce chaos within your schedule to make life more enjoyable.

Found something valuable in this chapter? Share it by taking a picture and tagging me on your Instagram stories @dejon_brooks!

My Goal of Meeting Two People a Day

Mid-2021, I moved from Atlanta to Provo, Utah.

As a joke to meet new people, I decided to pick up a goal of talking to two new people daily. As of this journal entry, I recently crossed the 1,000-person mark.

This may sound easy, but as I mentioned in the last section, I had to do the following:

- Talk for a minimum of two minutes
- Learn their name
- I couldn't count the same person twice

And to make this goal even more challenging, I couldn't cold approach anyone (with a few exceptions). Cold approaching is talking to someone randomly. Instead, I decided to make my approaches 100% organic.

I'll give you an example.

So, instead of working from my laptop in my apartment, I'll do it in a coffee shop. And guess what? Going outside the house increases the chances of me meeting someone naturally. You can't meet people inside the house.

Once I'm inside the coffee shop, I need to find a place to sit.

To do this, I'll purposely go up to someone sitting next to an empty seat and ask, "Is anyone sitting here?" anticipating a no.

If no were said, I'd use that as a gateway to start a light conversation while setting up my laptop. Depending on the circumstances, this conversation could go on for fifteen minutes or last a couple of seconds. That's my secret.

Every day, I plan my schedule so that I'm outside of the house most of the day. This helps me run into other organic situations, as explained in the example above. I did this goal for fun, but the benefits of doing it for three to four months have been INSANE.

Here are the benefits I noticed in my life:

- I went on lots of dates
- Got over stuttering/increased confidence
- It gave me the ability to talk to anyone

- Better at sales

- Made lots of cool friends and built unique social circles

- Mastered the art of going out alone

If your social/dating life sucks, I'd highly recommend picking up this goal! I wasn't anticipating those areas of my life to improve, but you'll see unbelievable results within the first fourteen days if you're consistent.

Inventing Tasks to Avoid the Important

I once had a crush on this girl back in high school. We both had an art class together. Instead of getting straight to the point and asking her on a date, I did the following to maximize the chances of getting a yes:

- Start working out to get a six-pack

- Get a few nice outfits and buy a chain

- Memorize lots of pickup jokes to appear funny

- Become a famous YouTuber

Shockingly, I achieved bullet point #4, but after months of trying to accomplish all these things, I thought I was ready to make my move.

When I arrived at my art class the next day, I shot my shot, and the unthinkable happened. I got rejected. The worst part about that rejection wasn't that I got rejected, but I wasted months of "preparing" just to hear a no. I could have saved a few months of my life by asking her on a date. Instead, I decided to invent unnecessary tasks that allowed me to avoid asking her out. I use this simple story as a reminder to get straight to the point whenever I do things.

Whenever I want to invent a task, I always ask myself, *Am I trying to avoid the big goal?* Here is another example…

My first business was a marketing agency. Instead of focusing on sales to get paying clients, I needed the following first to look "professional":

- Business cards
- Professional website (that was mobile friendly)
- Business address
- Flyers
- Business suit for meetings

Instead of focusing on getting clients, I spent time inventing new tasks to distract me from doing the important. This ultimately led to the failure of this business. Are you inventing tasks to avoid the essential things you should be focusing on?

If that's a yes, you must quickly swim out of the whirlpool and focus first on what is important. Doing this will save you time and allow you to achieve more.

Found something valuable in this chapter? Share it by taking a picture and tagging me on your Instagram stories @dejon_brooks!

The Importance of Sacrifice

At the beginning of 2020, I wanted to completely change my life to pull myself to the next level. To do this, I had to sacrifice the following for six months:

- Hanging with friends
- Dating
- Video games
- Partying
- *So* much more

While doing this, I was going 100% on building Trend Watchers in my parents' basement. During these six months, friends, family, and girls would try to drag me out of the house. But I refused. I wanted to turn my idea for Trend Watchers into reality.

And guess what? I did. I now have an automatic machine in the cloud that runs 24/7/365.

I could take a three-month vacation without looking at the thing, and everything will function normally. All because I decided to sacrifice six months of my life. Around my freshman year of high school, I dreamed of becoming a famous YouTuber.

All of my friends told me that I was going to fail. I sacrificed three hours every morning to get a video up for 100 days to prove them wrong. I refused to come outside and play until my daily video was up. No exceptions.

After grinding for 100 days in a row, I finally hit 250,000+ views in one day, which launched my crazy YouTube career. If you are between the ages of 18–30, you NEED to sacrifice a minimum of 6–12 months towards some big goal/project.

It doesn't matter what it is, but you'd be surprised how far you can get by giving something your 100%. As I was grinding in that basement, people told me not to try so hard and enjoy life. That is true, but I'd rather sacrifice a few months of my life for a lifetime of freedom and joy.

"He who chases two rabbits catches none." – Confucius

There is no other way around it. If you want it, you NEED to sacrifice.

Space

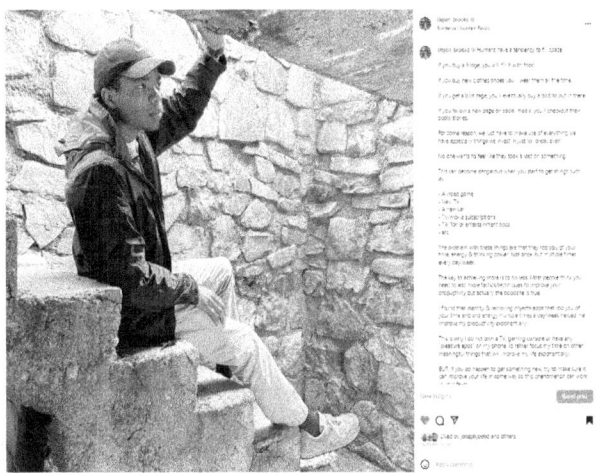

Humans tend to fill space.

If you buy a fridge, you will fill it with food.

If you buy new clothes/shoes, you'll always wear them.

If you get a birdcage, you'll eventually buy a bird to put in there.

If you follow a new page on social media, you'll check out their posts/stories.

For some reason, we have to use everything we have, especially things we invest in, to "break even." No one wants to feel like they took a loss on something.

This can become dangerous when you start to get things such as:

- A video game

- New TV
- A new car
- TV/movie subscriptions
- Entertainment apps

The problem with these things is that they rob you of your time, energy, and thinking power. Not once, but multiple times every day. The key to achieving more is to do less. Most people think you need to add more techniques to improve your productivity, but the opposite is true.

Identifying and removing things that rob you of your time and energy multiple times a day helped me improve my productivity exponentially.

This is why I do not own a TV or gaming console or have any "pleasure apps" on my phone. Instead, I focus my time on other meaningful things that will improve my life exponentially.

If you get something new, try to make sure it can improve your life so this phenomenon can work in your favor. I'll give you an example.

When I bought my first high ticket program for $2,000 at 18 years old, I gave that thing 100% of my attention. I wanted to break even on my investment, not because the information was good.

This goal accidentally made me plow through the entire program and consistently take action to where I now have my own online business, generating income 24/7 automatically.

How are you filling your space?

How I Improved My Sales Skills by Going on 28 Dates in 90 Days

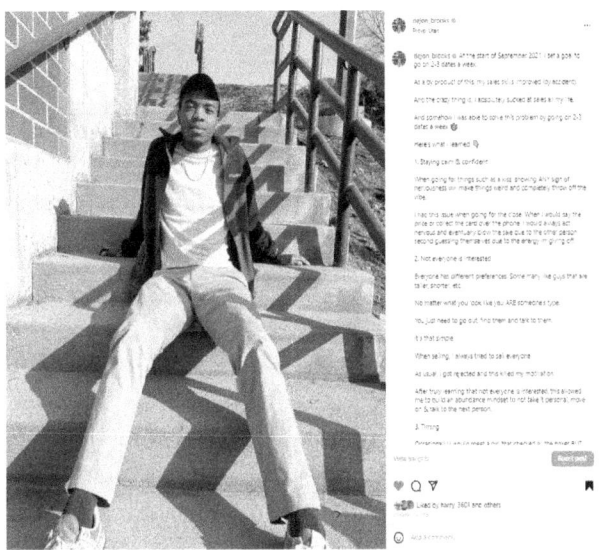

At the start of September 2021, I set a goal to go on two or three dates a week. As a by-product of this, my sales skills improved (by accident).

I've always sucked at sales my entire life. I've tried numerous things to fix it, but nothing worked. As a total accident, I solved this problem by going on a few dates a week. Here's what I learned…

1. Stay calm and confident

When going for things like a kiss, showing *any* sign of nervousness will make things weird and completely throw off the vibe.

I had this issue when going for the close. When I would say the price or collect the card over the phone, I would always act nervous and eventually blow the sale due to the other person second guessing themselves due to the energy I'm giving off.

2. Not everyone is interested

Everyone has different preferences—some like guys who are taller, shorter, etc. No matter what you look like, you *are* someone's type. You need to go out, find them, and talk to them. It's that simple.

When selling, I always tried to sell to everyone. As usual, I got rejected, and this killed my motivation. After truly learning that not everyone is interested, this allowed me to build an abundance mindset, not to take it personally, move on, and talk to the next person.

3. Timing

Occasionally, I would meet a girl who checked all the boxes, BUT

- She had a boyfriend
- Recently broke up with someone
- Was busy with life or school

This taught me the importance of timing.

When selling, I came across many people who lacked the money or were in a situation. After learning the timing lesson, I realized I had to adapt my offer (while showing empathy) to make it a win/win scenario for all.

4. Communication

Another thing I learned was how to communicate with total confidence. In the past, I was always afraid of offending someone I was talking to by questioning her stance on something. I also was super awkward on certain topics.

After going on all these dates, I learned how to ask good questions. This helped me on sales calls. Whenever I told a client they needed to change their life or business, I could do so without being awkward. If your sales skills suck, go on dates.

Found something valuable in this chapter? Share it by taking a picture and tagging me on your Instagram stories @dejon_brooks!

The Grass Is Greener Where You Water It

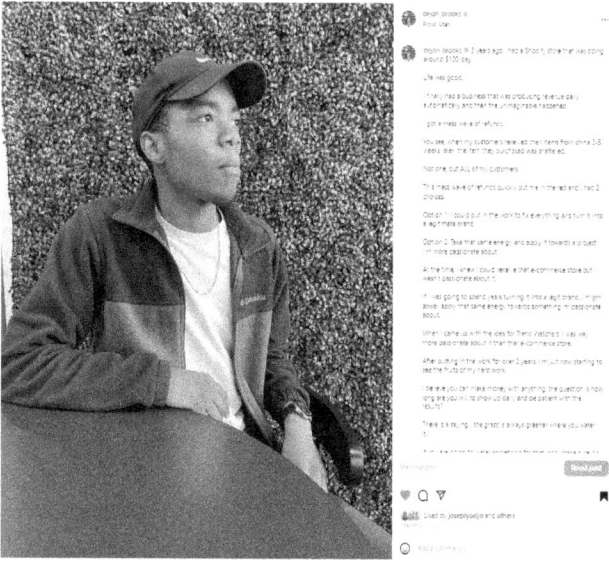

In high school, I had a Shopify store that was doing around $100/day. Life was good. I finally had a business that automatically produced revenue daily, and then the unimaginable happened. I got a mass wave of refunds.

You see, when my customers received their items from China three to five weeks later, the item they purchased was shattered. This happened to ALL of my customers. This mass wave of refunds quickly put me in the red, and I had two choices:

Option 1: I could put in the work to fix everything and turn it into a legitimate brand

Option 2: Take that same energy and apply it to a project I'm more passionate about

At the time, I knew I could revive that e-commerce store, but I wasn't passionate about it. If I was going to spend years turning it into a legit brand, I might as well apply that same energy toward something I'm passionate about.

When I came up with the idea for Trend Watchers, I was way more passionate about it than that e-commerce store. After putting in the work for over two years, I'm just now starting to see the fruits of my hard work.

You can make money with anything. The question is: How long are you willing to show up daily and be patient with the results?

The saying is, "The grass is always greener where you water it."

If you are going to water something for that long, make sure it brings fulfillment to your life. I was able to learn this lesson at 17 years old. Which grass are you going to water?

Are You Living or Existing?

Toward the beginning of 2021, something strange happened to my hands. My joints were swelling in both hands, looked red, and were sometimes hard to move. This was going off and on for a few weeks.

The same thing happened to me around December 2022–February 2023. After looking up my symptoms, it appears that I have a form of arthritis (haven't seen a doctor yet). After typing the words "arthritis cure" in Google, only to find out there isn't one, it got me thinking.

At this point, there are two paths I can take:

1) Worry about this thing I can't control 24/7 and be bitter about it.

2) Do my best to manage it and focus on living my life.

The easiest choice is to take option #1, but you'll end up living a life full of bitterness and regret. Option #2 is a bit painful initially, but as time goes on, you'll look back and start to view this obstacle as more of a blessing or defining moment of your life.

Our lives are like a half-finished book. The previous chapters may have been written, but we can write our current and future chapters. And if anything goes wrong, find ways to turn that negative into a positive.

If it is raining outside, don't be grumpy. Just go and dance in the rain. It is essential to stay positive, especially during those hard times. One of the biggest setbacks that took me forever to overcome was when my YouTube channel got demonetized. I easily lost tens of thousands of dollars due to this, and there was nothing I could do.

Instead of going back to my usual ways and dropping the whole "make money online" concept, I found a way to create something new (Trend Watchers) with *way* more potential.

I also use my demonetized story every time I explain Trend Watchers to someone to show them that I found another opened door after one was closed in front of me.

Are you living or existing?

Found something valuable in this chapter? Share it by taking a picture and tagging me on your Instagram stories @dejon_brooks!

It's Your Job to Ask and Their Job to Say No

One random weekend, I wanted to visit somewhere new, so I visited the University of Utah's campus in Salt Lake City. I planned on taking the train from Provo, getting off in Salt Lake City, and then walking directly east 'til I reached the campus. This walking distance looked very short from a map point of view, but I didn't realize it was 3.5 miles long (one way).

Once I arrived, I spent a few hours on the campus and began my 3.5-mile journey back to the train station. Roughly ten minutes into my journey back, I saw a bus stopped on the roadside.

I was going to keep walking but decided to give it a shot and ask for a ride. It turns out it was "Free Fare February," so I was able to ride along for free. I saved myself from walking an extra three miles. All I had to do was ask.

Later that week, I was on a call with a potential client. About fifteen minutes into the call, I decided to tell him the price and go for the close. (It felt like good timing). Initially, I was nervous because it was off-script, but I still went for it. To my surprise, he said yes, and I was able to close a $3,000 package.

What did I learn from these two experiences? Be bold and ask. Even if you are not sure the other person will say yes, ask anyway. Suppose they say yes? Well, good for you. If they say no, it won't be the end of the world. When we hear no, we are ALWAYS pushed in the direction we are supposed to go.

"It's your job to ask and their job to say no." – Dejon Brooks

Managing Your Emotions

Around the age of 8, I had a lot of energy.

This, combined with anger issues, led to me becoming very destructive. I would:

- Break toys

- Break windows

- Write on walls

- Do dumb stuff at school that would get me suspended

This all doesn't sound *that* bad, but it was horrible back then. My lowest point was when I fought a police officer in the sixth grade and got expelled from middle school. After that incident, I had to see a counselor. A few visits in, it finally hit me, and I was able to snap out of it.

I remember sitting in the chair, talking with my anger management counselor. She kept asking me *a lot* of questions, and I remember thinking, *This is bs*. It felt so unproductive, spewing out my emotional fuel to her.

After that realization, I started telling her what she wanted to hear to get out of those sessions faster. Once I "graduated" from anger management counseling, I started applying this "emotional fuel" in the form of anger toward a productive project. This is how I began my first venture of selling Roblox accounts.

After teaching myself how to channel my emotions towards something productive, and I started seeing results, the quality of my life began to improve exponentially.

I used this same energy to:

- Become a famous YouTuber
- Start and scale Trend Watchers from scratch
- And literally achieve any goal I want

Without this emotional fuel, there was no way I could achieve the things I wanted. I could still go for it, but I couldn't do it well if I spewed out my emotional fuel. There is a time and place when you should share your emotions, but don't spew your emotional fuel to everyone.

Figure out ways to take some of that fuel to accelerate toward your ambitions and hobbies. Emotional fuel is like steam. You can't get rid of it; you can only manage it. The best way to use it is to channel it towards something productive. I know I'm repeating myself, but this is one of the superpowers I use to plow through the ups and downs of entrepreneurship.

Hiding from Your Life

Recently, I caught myself hiding from my life. When hiding from your life, you know EXACTLY what you need to do to get to the next level but choose not to. You look for ways to:

- Make excuses
- Put tasks off for tomorrow
- Talk yourself out of taking action

People do this for various reasons, but I noticed I tend to do this because I am afraid of change. The uncertainty of going to higher highs makes me scared deep down, which causes me to self-sabotage. Looking back on the past, I always sabotaged myself like this before I got a massive breakthrough.

This brings me to my next question: How do you fix this problem? In life, we all love quick fixes to big and small problems. We want to use a specific life hack or app that can take all of our problems away, but unfortunately, on this issue, the only way to work around it is to push through the pain and do the work.

My favorite technique for doing this is to chunk out my work across multiple weeks on a daily level. This productivity hack has helped me climb massive mountains within my business one step at a time without overwhelming myself. If you ever catch yourself hiding from your life, try the following:

Step 1: Recognize that you are hiding from your life

Step 2: Identity what you need to do to turn it around and reach your goals/ambitions

Step 3: Do the work

Are you hiding from your life?

The Power of Thinking Trips

During my high school years, I was obsessed with Tai Lopez. I loved his content on YouTube and would watch it religiously. In one of his uploads, he made a video about the importance of thinking trips. Thinking trips are where you go somewhere roughly 100+ miles away from your home and think.

Thinking trips are powerful because when you put yourself in an unfamiliar place, you become more aware of your surroundings. This makes it easier to relax, get your mind off things, and tap into your creativity. Thinking trips have helped me:

- Figure out solutions to personal problems
- Figure out solutions to business problems
- Clear my head
- Seek inspiration
- Allow me to see things from a new perspective

When I go on thinking trips, I always bring a blank sheet of paper, a pen, and a clipboard. I next write down all of my problems with three empty bullet points under the issues. Why are these bullet points empty?

You see, we humans need to fill space. If we buy an empty birdcage, we'll eventually buy a bird. If we buy a TV, we will watch it. If we get an air fryer, we will buy food to cook in it. I use this same logic for solving my problems.

By writing it down, I ALWAYS find a way to fill the space (solve my problem) naturally. I use this technique combined with thinking trips repeatedly to solve challenging problems in my personal and business life.

Why You Should Join a Cult

One of the best life hacks I've ever done was joining an internet cult throughout my early years of entrepreneurship. When I say cult, I'm not talking about some weird group worshipping some fantasy god or object. I'm talking about cults centered around good causes/end goals that also allow you to grow exponentially due to the culture.

One of the first cults I was in was an online video game called *Goodgame Empire*. Within the game was an alliance I completely admired. I loved this alliance because:

1. They were the top alliance in the game.
2. All of their players game from a fitness forum, so they were always in shape and talking about lifting and self-improvement.
3. They spoke whatever was on their minds and went for what they wanted.
4. When wartime came, they coordinated *really* well and gave it their all with high spirits.
5. They had a fantastic alliance culture (memes, jokes, etc.).

Seeing these things as an outsider made me want to join their alliance (and I eventually did!). I was so obsessed with this alliance that I ended up taking some of the attributes I picked up in this group and started applying them to the projects I was working on in real life. For example, I wanted to become a famous YouTuber, so as I posted content daily, I used their mindset to build game plans and eventually pass my competitors.

The point of joining internet cults is not to meet other people but to extract that mindset and apply it to your personal goals and ambitions.

Taking this mindset (it doesn't matter who you get it from) allows you to plow through tough times effortlessly. Challenging times are when most people quit. To succeed in anything, it's going to take time and experiencing hard patches. If you can endure long enough, you'll eventually make it, and I found that the mindset good cults provide allows me to do this effortlessly. Examples of good cults are:

- Accountability groups
- High-level paid communities
- Self-improvement groups

Motivation will take you around the corner. Discipline will take you a couple of hundred miles. But the mindset extracted from a good cult will take you thousands of miles (from my experience). This is my #1 productivity hack.

Conviction

I've been consuming Alex Hormozi's content lately, and something he said hit me in the spot. The topic he was talking about was conviction. Long story short, conviction is being able to talk about something with 100% certainty. The only way to get this level of certainty is to do the thing yourself.

In my case with Trend Watchers, I wasn't actively applying the trends myself on YouTube. I was just selling the trends along with the framework to my customers.

The stuff I was selling worked, but for some reason, some users had an easier time than others when applying trends to YouTube. The difference between these clients was their experience with making content. To solve this issue, I took the time to completely redo my course and make it easy to where a 5-year-old could follow along. On top of this, I also:

- Created templates
- Created frameworks
- Created help centers
- Created easy-to-access support lines

This allowed me to have a better product that could help my clients get results. Because of this, I can now sell to potential customers over the phone with conviction. I'm so convinced that my service works, I now offer people a thirty-day refund if our systems don't work for them (which I've never done before). Making this change within my business caused me to:

- Become customer-obsessed

- Become preoccupied with watching clients get results

- Focus on one product and get rid of everything else

- Track everything

- Continually improving my reduction instead of just maintaining

- Be open to feedback

These are the attributes I need to have as a CEO to take my business to the next level.

Found something valuable in this chapter? Share it by taking a picture and tagging me on your Instagram stories @dejon_brooks!

Stepping Your Sh!t Up

I've been surrounding myself with higher-level people recently. This has been done both in-person and through other forms, such as content. To take it to the next level, I'm sticking with people around my age bracket of 21–30.

Seeing people around my age killing it forces me to "Step my sh!t up." Seriously, I was with a friend this past Sunday, and he was walking me through the house that he owned. He was showing me all of the renovations he was making, and I was really happy for him. Instead of being envious of his progress, I took it as inspiration to go harder on my grind.

I thought I was doing good with my business until I came across Alex Hormozi's content. He told me to step up my service by providing more value and charging people more for it. Because of this, I increased my prices from $500 to $1,500 and $3,000 to $5,000.

I was just with a friend about a month ago. He made me step my game up as far as traveling and trying new experiences. Two weeks before that experience, I helped a friend propose to his girlfriend. That was a reality check that I needed to step myself up to become a person worthy of a healthy, fun marriage.

I follow a lot of coaches and authors on Instagram. Seeing these people signing their books, getting high-level press, and getting tons of sales makes me want to write more chapters each week to get my book *Bootstrapped* out. I also went to a networking event where Jess, the owner of Mixhers, was speaking. Her company's primary source of growth was leveraging influencers/affiliates and treating them like family.

This inspired me to step my game up, double down on my affiliate program, and give them all the resources they need to succeed. If you struggle with motivation, surround yourself with people who have already made it.

The Curse of Options

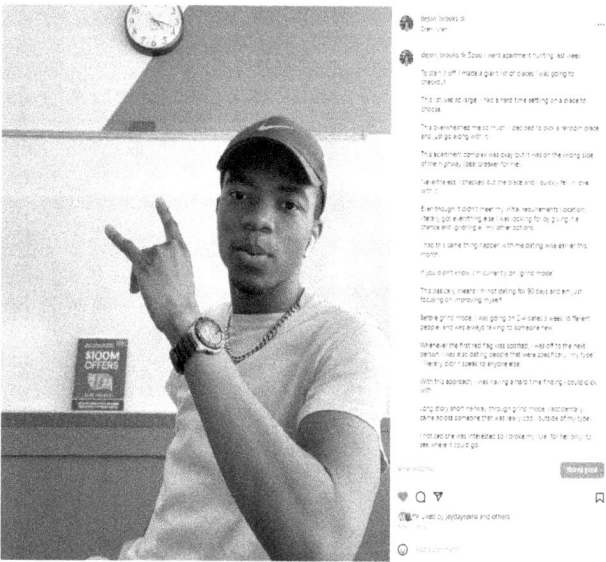

I went apartment hunting during the summer of 2022. The first thing I did was create a giant list of places I would check out. This list was so large that I had a hard time picking a location. This overwhelmed me so much that I decided to pick a random place and use that as a starting point.

With the pictures provided online, the apartment complex looked halfway decent. It was also on the wrong side of town, but I checked it out anyway. Long story short, I ended up falling in love with it. Even though it didn't meet my initial requirements (location), I got everything else I was looking for by giving it a chance and ignoring all my other options.

I had this same thing happen to me dating-wise around this time. At the time, I was currently in "grind mode." This means I'm not dating for ninety days and just focusing on improving myself. Before grind mode, I was going on two to four dates a week (with different people) and was always talking to someone new.

I was off to the next person whenever the first red flag was spotted. I was also dating people that were specifically "my type." I didn't speak to anyone else. With this approach, I had a hard time finding someone I could click with. Halfway through grind mode, I accidentally came across someone who was cool (outside of my type). I noticed she was interested, so I broke my rule (for her only) to see where it could go.

As we went on five dates in two weeks, I discovered so many beautiful attributes about her. Had I been dating two or three other people simultaneously, I would have never found these amazing attributes about her. Luckily, she caught me in the middle of grind mode. Unfortunately, we didn't work out, but it was fascinating how my results changed when I focused on one person at a time and was open minded.

If you're struggling with something, try reducing your options and open your mind a bit.

Found something valuable in this chapter? Share it by taking a picture and tagging me on your Instagram stories @dejon_brooks!

Gratitude Journaling

About every few months or so, I like to pick up a new habit to change things in my life. I've been following Hamza on YouTube for the past few months. I like watching his content cause he focuses on men's self-improvement. I specifically learned from him the importance of daily gratitude journaling.

He inspired me to write down five things I'm grateful for at the end of each day. To make gratitude journaling more meaningful, I also enforced the following rules:

- I don't write the same thing twice when stating things I'm grateful for
- I write my wins for the day
- I write what frustrated me
- I write about what I can do to improve myself for tomorrow
- I also write down what I can do tomorrow to make it successful

I've tried keeping a gratitude journal, but I have always failed. I would always give up after about a week. By forcing myself to do it for sixty days, I've been able to:

- See the good during my bad days
- Track and accumulate my small daily wins
- Understand and track the patterns of my feelings and mood swings
- Build my journal on a daily level
- Learned how to be grateful during both good and bad times

If you are looking for a new good habit, I highly recommend you try keeping a gratitude journal. You may not see any results within the first few weeks, but once you do, there is no going back!

Shatter Your Life

Are you in your comfort zone? Are you not challenging yourself?

Do the days seem to blend? Are you spinning your tires in life?

If you answered yes to any of these, you need to take your life and smash it to pieces. No matter how excellent or comfortable your situation is, you must break your life into pieces. Especially when you are young.

Once this is done, you next need to ask yourself, *What do I want to do with my life?* or *What type of life do I want to live five, ten, fifteen years from now?* Too often, people spend a large chunk of their lives doing something they don't like. There's nothing wrong with doing this for a short period to straighten out finances, but eventually, you need to transition towards something that will satisfy you.

I have always had a passion for men's self-improvement. Instead of dreaming of becoming a men's self-improvement coach, I just smashed my life and am now chasing that goal. When breaking and crafting your new life, I love to hit the following areas specifically:

- Where I live
- How I look
- My social circle
- Content I consume
- Music I listen to
- My goals in life
- Plus lots of other small areas in my life

Five years ago, I was listening to a podcast. I forgot what they were talking about, but this line hit me: "It's not that you are depressed; therefore, your life is static. It's the other way around. Your life is static; therefore, you are depressed."

Once I heard that line and applied it, my depression and feelings of hopelessness were solved. Whenever I feel it is coming back, I always change a variable in my life. Most of the time, I'll change one or two variables every month or so. About every year, I'll do a major one where I shatter my entire life and completely rebuild it.

Does your life feel static? Try smashing it to pieces. Remember, there is no such thing as maintenance. Either you are moving forward or backward.

Found something valuable in this chapter? Share it by taking a picture and tagging me on your Instagram stories @dejon_brooks!

The Importance of Self-Promotion

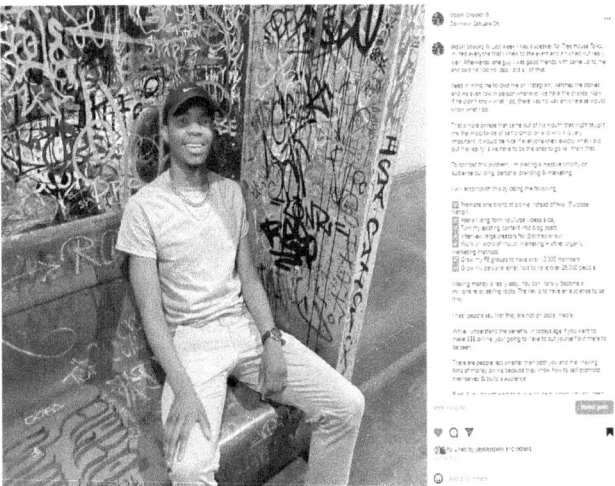

Last week, I was a speaker for Tree House Talks. I invited everyone I knew to the event, which turned out really well! Afterward, one guy I was good friends with came up and said he had no idea I did all of that.

Keep in mind this guy follows me on Instagram (which showcases my entire business), watches the stories, and we even talk in person whenever we can. Now, if he didn't know what I do, there was no way anyone else would know what I do. That simple phrase that came out of his mouth that night taught me the importance of self-promotion and why it is essential. It would be nice if everyone knew what I did, but the reality is that we have to be the ones to tell them.

To combat this problem, I prioritized audience-building, personal branding, and marketing. I accomplished this by doing the following:

- Post one long-form YouTube video a day

- Turn my existing content into blog posts

- Interview large creators for @entrepreneur

- Work on word-of-mouth marketing + other organic marketing methods

- Grow my FB groups to have over 10,000 members

- Grow my email lists to have over 25,000 people

Making money is easy. You can become a millionaire by selling rocks. The key is to have an audience to sell it to.

I hear people say that they are not on social media. While I understand the benefits, in today's age, if you want to make money online, you need to put yourself out there to be seen. There are people less smart than you and me, making tons of money online because they know how to self-promote and build an audience. Even if you do not want to own an online business, you must promote yourself to get that job, make friends, etc.

It would be nice if this stuff could come to us naturally, but we must do the ugly work of self-promotion so others know we exist. What are you doing to make yourself seen?

Never Settle

I recently hiked Mount Timpanogos with a group of friends. It was a fifteen-miles round trip and took us all morning and afternoon to complete. I'm pretty fit, so it wasn't bad for me. As we kept getting closer to the top (with the way we took), there were a few extremely sketchy points. Usually, I would go into panic mode, walking next to high drop-offs while walking on ice, but I was able to stay calm and push through with total ease.

About thirty minutes later, we reached this point near the top that had an AMAZING view. It was not the top, but the view was phenomenal. You could see everything in all directions. In our group, one of the guys was not a fan of heights. Because of this fear, he decided to stay at this point and not proceed. He decided to settle. The path to the top of the mountain was another .30 miles away and looked unsafe from where we were at the time. I *almost* joined him but decided to push through because of the dangers of settling.

When you settle on the big things/goals in life, you won't regret it too badly, but it will slowly eat away your self-esteem with time. Self-esteem is important because that's how you tell yourself that you can do hard/big things. Sure, this was just a hike, but the good/bad effects of this can pour into other areas of your life. Literally, that same day, I decided to go dancing with another group of friends.

As we were dancing, I saw this group of girls that were way out of my league. They were dancing towards the back of the room in their own circle. Because of my win earlier that day of summiting that mountain, it gave me the confidence to go up and approach this group of girls, and we had a great time!

I could have settled and had a blast with my group, but because I knew I could successfully do things outside of my comfort zone, I approached the group. Stay focused on the big goals in life, and don't settle. If you do settle, it will slowly lower your self-esteem and lurk into other areas of your life.

Turn Everything You Touch into Gold

One skill I've been mastering is turning everything I touch into gold. I first heard of this concept from a video I saw from Tai Lopez a few years ago. The areas I've specifically been applying this concept to are:

- My conversations with other people
- The way I execute my work
- Doing service for others

I'll break each one down.

1) Conversations with other people

The point of turning everything you touch into gold is to leave the interaction better than how you first found it. When it comes to talking to other people, I love doing this naturally by:

- Smiling
- Being enthusiastic
- Listening and being interested in what the other person is saying
- Always providing value without expecting anything in return
- Learning their name, interests, and where they are from
- Asking meaningful questions and diving deep into their interests

2) Execution of my work

As I develop my products and services, I love turning that into gold by listening to customer feedback and going above and beyond to over-deliver results. I also love going the extra mile by talking one-on-one with my customers to understand their needs.

3) Service to others

When serving others, I like doing small, simple things unexpectedly. It always catches people off guard and almost always makes their day.

How do you turn everything you touch into gold?

Found something valuable in this chapter? Share it by taking a picture and tagging me on your Instagram stories @dejon_brooks!

Grind It Out

Recently, I've adjusted some of my long-term goals due to a change of passion/priorities. To reach these new goals, I had to create new daily routines. The purpose of these routines is to help me move one step closer to my big goals every day. I've been implementing these routines for about two months, and it's starting to feel repetitive.

One thing I love about chunking out my work is that it allows me to reach any goal by breaking it down into daily tasks. On the downside, these daily tasks can start to feel repetitive, and some days I do not feel like doing the work. To fight against this instinct of choosing comfort over work, I think of the following things:

1) Helping your older self out

We all will get old one day. The best time to prepare is now while we are still in our youth and full of energy. One exercise I enjoy doing is thinking of how my previous self sacrificed comfort to help me get to where I am today.

2) Regret

Failure is temporary, but regret is forever. Sure, throwing in the towel would be nice, but what would have happened if you kept showing up for another few months? Would you have reached your goal? This is the part that makes regret so painful in the long run. I would rather fail and lose money and time than spend the rest of my life wondering what would have happened.

3) Other people are counting on me

Do you have a spouse, kids, or family that relies on you? I love using these important people to help me plow through the boring work. I love imagining the new life I can provide for these people once I reach my desired goal. I also enjoy imagining my new life after reaching my new goal.

Things will get hard no matter what gender, profession, or age you are. We need to suck up the pain and grind it out. It would be nice if everything were easy, but the reality is it is not, and sometimes we have to push through.

1 Year of Living on My Own

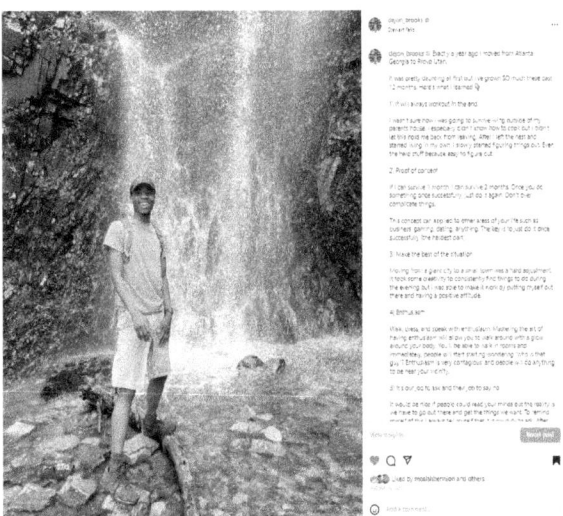

Moving out of my parents' house for a year was a scary change, but it was worth it. It was initially daunting, but I've grown *so* much within twelve months. Here's what I learned:

1) It will always work out in the end

I wasn't sure how I would survive living outside of my parents' house. I didn't know how to cook, but I didn't let this keep me from leaving. After leaving the nest and living on my own, I slowly started figuring things out. Even the hard stuff became easy to figure out.

2) Proof of concept

If I can survive one month, I can survive two months. Once you do something successfully, do it again. Don't overcomplicate things. This concept can be applied to other areas of your life, such as business, gaming, dating, etc. The key is to do it once successfully (the most challenging part).

3) Make the best of the situation

Moving from a big city to a small town was a hard adjustment. It took some creativity to consistently find things to do during the evening, but I was able to make it work by putting myself out there and having a positive attitude.

4) Enthusiasm

Walk, dress, and speak with enthusiasm. Mastering the art of having enthusiasm will allow you to walk around with a glow around your body. You'll be able to walk into rooms, and immediately, people will start wondering, *Who is that guy?* Enthusiasm is very contagious, and people will do anything to be in your vicinity.

5) It's our job to ask and their job to say no

It would be nice if people could read your mind, but we must go out there and get what we want. To remind myself of this, I always tell myself that it is my duty to ask. After that, the other person is responsible for telling me no (worst-case scenario). You'll be surprised at what you can get away with.

6) Journal, journal, journal!

Time is like water running through our fingers. It goes by so fast. Make sure you keep a journal and take *tons* of pictures. Your older self will thank you!

What did you learn during your first year outside the bird's nest? If you haven't left yet, I'd highly recommend doing so!

Volume Guarantees Luck

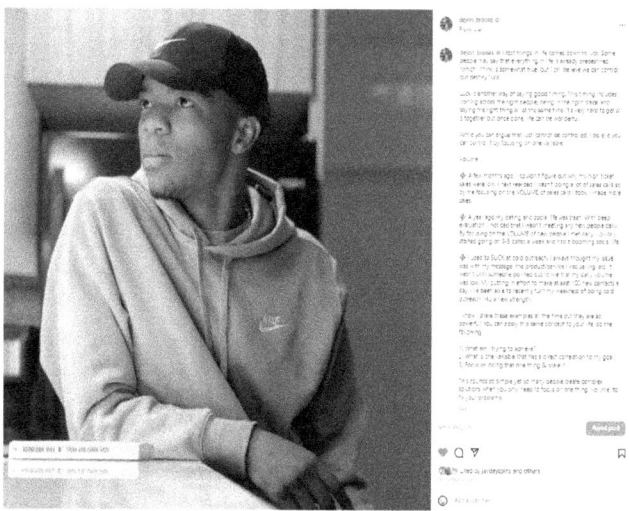

Most things in life come down to luck. Some people may say that everything in life is already predestined (which is somewhat true), but I still believe we can control our destiny/luck. Luck is another way of saying good timing. This timing includes coming across the right people, being in the right place, and saying the right thing all at the same time. It's tough trying to get all three together, but once done, life is wonderful.

While you can argue that luck cannot be controlled, you can control it by focusing on one variable: volume.

 A few months ago, I couldn't figure out why my high ticket sales were low. I next realized I wasn't doing a lot of sales calls, so by focusing on the VOLUME of sales calls I took, I made more sales. A year ago, my dating and social life was trash. After an in-depth evaluation, I noticed I wasn't meeting any new

160

people daily. By focusing on the VOLUME of new people I met daily, I quickly started going on three to five dates a week and had a thriving social life.

I used to SUCK at cold outreach. I always thought my issue was with my message, the product/service I was selling, etc. It wasn't until someone pointed out that my daily volume was low. By putting in the effort to make at least 100 new contacts a day, I've recently turned my weakness of doing cold outreach into a new strength. I share these examples all the time, but they are so powerful! You can apply this same concept to your life by:

1) Asking yourself, *What am I trying to achieve?*

2) Asking yourself, *What is one variable that directly correlates to my goal?*

3) Focusing on doing that one thing and scaling it.

This sounds so simple, yet so many people create complex solutions when you only need to focus on one thing (volume) to fix your problems.

How to Get over a Breakup

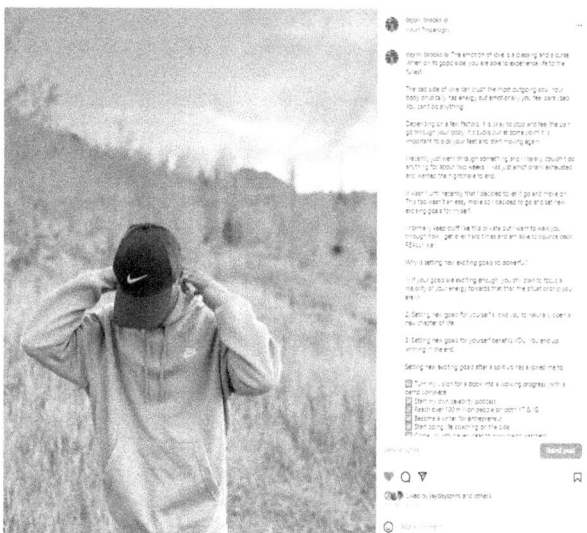

The emotion of love is a blessing and a curse. On the good side, you can experience life to the fullest. But the wrong side of love can crush the most outgoing soul. Your body physically has energy, but emotionally, you feel paralyzed. You can't do anything.

Depending on a few factors, stopping and feeling the pain go through your body is okay. It sucks, but at some point, it's essential to pick up your feet and start moving again. At the time of this writing, I recently went through something and couldn't do anything for about two weeks. I was just emotionally exhausted and wanted the nightmare to end. I next decided to let it go and move on. This was a challenging move, but I went and set new, exciting goals for myself. I usually keep stuff like this private, but I want to walk you through how I get over hard times and bounce back.

Why is setting new, exciting goals so powerful?

1) If your goals are exciting enough, you'll focus most of your energy on that rather than the situation you are in.

2) Setting new goals for yourself allows you to open a new chapter of life naturally.

3) Setting new goals for yourself benefits YOU. You end up winning in the end.

It sucks going through heartbreak. Instead of using that emotional energy towards destructive things, apply it towards something positive, such as a new goal.

Found something valuable in this chapter? Share it by taking a picture and tagging me on your Instagram stories @dejon_brooks!

Travel the World

Towards the end of 2022, I wanted to take a mini road trip to a hot spring about two hours south of where I live. As a friend and I started driving to this hot spring, I realized that I had never been twenty minutes south of where I lived in the entire year and a half I lived here in Provo.

This insight completely shocked me and inspired me to start traveling more. When it comes to traveling, what's the #1 reason people don't travel?

Money.

I used to be the same way until I realized that money comes and goes. There will always be more money to make tomorrow. This doesn't mean you should spend all of your money or go heavily into debt.

I was at a white elephant gift exchange, and I had the option to steal and secure a set of luxury mugs or a $25 Visa gift card (second steal for both of them). At first, I was going to go for the $25 gift card, but I remembered that money comes and goes. If I were to take the mugs, I would always remember the memory of how I got them each time I used them.

One fascinating insight I noticed from my recent travels within the past two years was that by traveling, I was *always* able to get my money back through the ideas generated while I was away. When you put yourself in a new environment, all of your senses are activated. It always allows you to see the world from a different perspective and think differently.

This change in your thought process makes it easier to think outside the box and develop the most *amazing* ideas. Don't be afraid to spend money and time traveling.

Never Feel Ashamed When Asking for Help

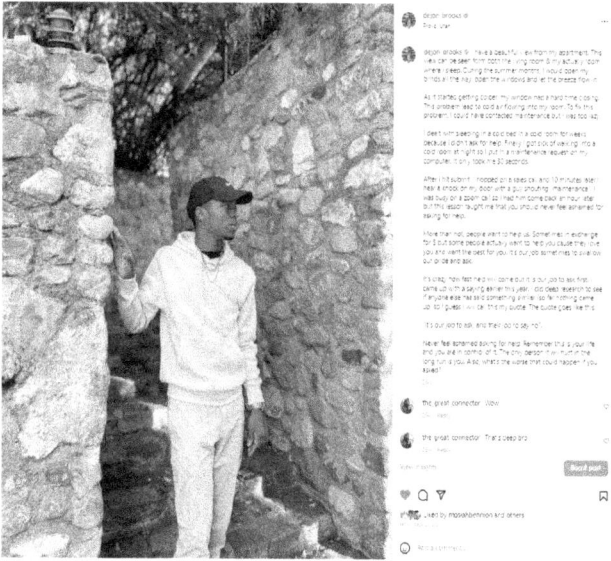

I have a beautiful view from my apartment. This view can be seen from both the living room and bedroom. During the summer, I would open the windows and let the breeze flow in. As it started getting colder, my window had a hard time closing. This problem caused cold air to start flowing into my room. To fix this problem, I could have contacted maintenance, but I was too lazy.

I dealt with sleeping in a cold bed in a cold room for weeks because I didn't ask for help. Finally, I got sick of walking into a cold room at night, so I made a maintenance request on my computer. It only took me thirty seconds. After I hit *Submit,* I hopped on a sales call, and ten minutes later, I heard a knock on my door with a guy shouting, "Maintenance!" I was busy on a Zoom call, so I had him come back an hour later to fix the window. This story is so simple, but it taught me that you should never feel ashamed for asking for help.

More than not, people want to help us. Sometimes, in exchange for money, but some people actually want to help you 'cause they love you and want the best for you. It's our job sometimes to swallow our pride and ask. It's wild how fast help will come, but it is our job to ask first. As I always say,

"It's our job to ask and their job to say no."

Never feel ashamed asking for help. Remember, this is your life, and you control it. The only person it will hurt in the long run is you. Also, what's the worst that could happen if you asked?

Chase Mountaintops, Not Money

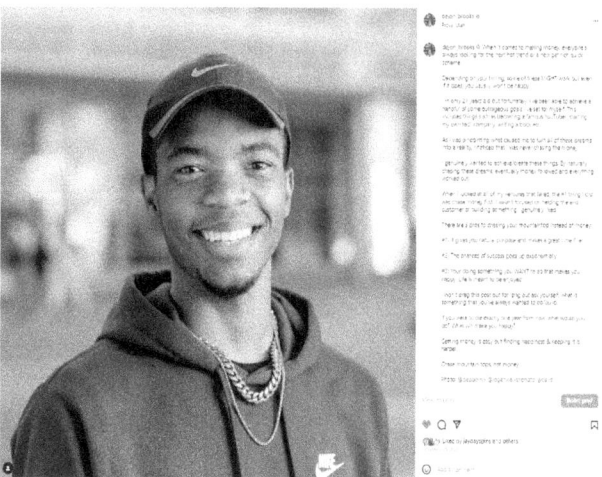

When it comes to making money, everyone's always looking for the next hot trend or a new get-rich-quick scheme. Depending on your timing, some of these *might* work, but you usually won't be happy even if it does. I'm only 21 years old (at the time of this writing), but fortunately, I've achieved a handful of some outrageous goals I've set for myself.

As I was pinpointing what caused me to turn all of these dreams into reality, I noticed that I was never chasing the money. I genuinely wanted to create and achieve these things. By naturally chasing these dreams, money eventually followed, and everything worked out. When I looked at all of my failed ventures, the #1 thing I did was chase money first. I wasn't focused on helping the end customer or building something I genuinely liked.

There are three pros to chasing your mountaintop instead of money:

1) It gives you a natural purpose and makes a great time filler

2) The chances of success increase exponentially

3) You're doing something you *want* to do that makes you happy. Life is meant to be enjoyed

I won't drag this section out for long, but ask yourself, what is something that you've always wanted to do? What would you do if you were to die exactly one year from now? What will make you happy? Getting money is easy, but finding happiness and keeping it is more challenging. Chase mountaintops, not money.

Found something valuable in this chapter? Share it by taking a picture and tagging me on your Instagram stories @dejon_brooks!

Invest in Your Family 'Cause Family Is Forever

I was on my monthly call with my OG accountability partner a few weeks ago. We've held each other accountable for the past two years (as of this writing). In this call, he told me about how business was booming, dating life was at an all-time high, and everything was going well. There was one problem, though. He wasn't happy with his life. He felt like there was something deeper he was missing.

He next told me he started spending more time with his family. This includes his mom, dad, sister, and extended family. I won't share all his business here, but long story short, he told me that money, girls, friends, and everything else is temporary. These people and things come and go.

But family is forever, so invest in them. I always knew family is forever, but hearing the words "invest in them" hit me differently. I've been pondering on this discussion for the past month, thinking about different ways I can further invest in my family. Here's what I came up with:

- Use them as a resource when I'm not sure how to do something
- Listen to their problems and struggles
- Look for different ways to maintain peace and serve one another
- Uplift and praise one another
- Plus, so much more!

Now, I'm not saying go and ditch your friends and other relationships, but continue to invest in them, too. Those relationships are just as valuable as the relationship between you and your family, but don't forget to invest in your family as well. For those that might have some heat with their mother, father, etc., go to whoever you define as family and invest in them.

There are four different types of capital that everyone NEEDS. I will write more about these in my next book:

- Emotional capital
- Financial capital
- Social capital
- Personal capital

Investing in your family allows you to build emotional capital. This capital is a handy resource to tap into for emotional support and advice (when needed). Family is forever, so invest in them!

The Older You Get, the More You'll Understand

Always ask questions. Even if you know everything, keep asking. Asking questions will not only allow you to learn more but will also help you understand the reason why people do what they do. You see, everyone has a sob story. Or, in other words, a defining moment.

This moment/event usually occurred in the past and typically affects how we think, see, and interact with the world. Unfortunately, most of these sob stories are negative. It can include things such as:

- A breakup
- Bad family relationships
- Traumatic events
- A massive failure
- And so many other scenarios/situations

Why is understanding people's defining moments so crucial? It allows us to see the big picture and know how to navigate the situation to where all parties are satisfied. I've recently figured this out through both business and dating, but I'll share my insights from dating for this chapter. Learning how to communicate and asking deep, inspiring questions to understand why the people I date do what they do has allowed me to:

- Be vulnerable and strengthen our connection
- Be more patient
- Be more understanding
- Be more of a listener

Having the big picture makes it easier to maintain the qualities listed above when issues arise. This is why I always love spending the first couple of dates discussing deep subjects. There is beauty in getting to know someone's story and understanding how their life experiences have shaped them into the person they are today. As I get older, I'm starting to value deep conversations and connections more and more.

My challenge for you is to talk less. Always ask questions and try to understand why people do what they do (it's usually different from what you think it is). Once you figure out why, you'll be amazed.

"The older you get, the more you understand."

—   Criss Jami

Always Push Forward

No matter how good your situation is, you always want to strive for better. Go out there and learn new skills, go somewhere new, or switch up your social circle. Forcing yourself to get into new things will allow you to grow.

As they always say, sharks die when they stop swimming. I am at a reasonably okay point in my life, but I CANNOT stop swimming. When setting my goals for December 2022, I told myself I wanted to level up and learn some new skills. I sat and thought about it for a day or two, and this is what I came up with...

1) Learn how to master making short-form videos (TikToks and reels)

I'm currently in the process of creating shortvideotrends.co. This software aims to pull trending sounds and songs from TikTok to help creators go viral. To best fulfill this purpose, I must be good at TikTok.

This is why I am looking into mastering the platform, as well as a few others. On top of this, I can also use short-form content to grow my audience and acquire new customers.

Learning this skill will allow me to:

- Get good at filming short videos that are engaging
- Master a new marketing channel
- Learn how to tell short stories in 5–10 seconds

2) Learn how to break even with paid advertising

When taking my finances to the next level, learning how to run paid ads that can break even is the last link in my chain. Adding this skill set to my tool belt is going to be *extremely* valuable.

Taking the time to learn this skill will allow me to:

- Master another marketing channel
- Learn how to set up advanced tracking
- Learn how to create full-stack funnels

3) Polish my copywriting skills

I'm preparing to write another book soon. To prepare, I've been making it a goal to write every day. This includes trying different styles, using emotion, contrast, etc.

I don't want to go on forever, but I did this to improve myself right before the new year (2023). Before you enter any new year, ask yourself:

- Am I learning new skills?
- Am I challenging myself?
- Am I constantly getting out of my comfort zone?
- Am I pushing myself forward?

Found something valuable in this chapter? Share it by taking a picture and tagging me on your Instagram stories @dejon_brooks!

Building an Abundance Mindset

I was listening to a podcast, and to be honest, I spaced out. It was pretty much background noise. But there was one part that caught my attention. This part of the podcast talks about how Adobe conducted a study from 2020 to 2023 on how many people joined the creator economy. This number was 100 million.

When I heard that, my jaw dropped. One hundred million people are my ideal customers for Trend Watchers (creators). But I still couldn't wrap my mind around that number. Fast-forward a few hours later, I'm on an airplane from Salt Lake City to Atlanta.

During the flight, I woke up and looked out the window. We just happened to be over Memphis, Tennessee. I specifically remember looking at all the night lights and saying, "That's easily 500,000 people." This further opened my eyes to the amount of abundance there is out there. This is why I love going on thinking trips. The point of thinking trips is to write out my problems and go to a new place that forces me to think differently.

This shift in thoughts allows me to build an abundance mindset and the confidence needed to work through whatever issue I'm trying to solve. Why is having an abundance mindset so powerful?

Answer: It gives you confidence, and confidence attracts success.

I can only think of two ways to build a natural abundance mindset:

1) Surround yourself with others who are where you want to be

Surrounding yourself with other people who are further along the path than you is a great way to build an abundance mindset. It mentally helps you comprehend that it is POSSIBLE!

2) Increase your options

Increasing your options puts you in a calm and confident mindset. If you screw it up, there will be more opportunities ahead.

The Best Teacher of Reality Is Reality

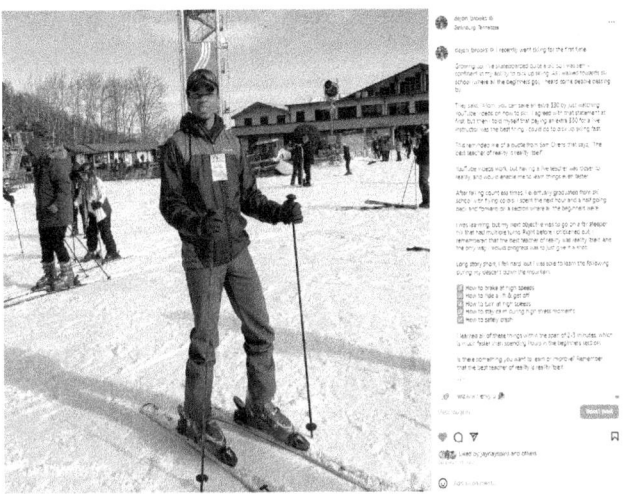

I recently went skiing for the first time. Growing up, I skateboarded quite a bit, so I was semi-confident in picking up skiing. As I walked towards ski school (where all the beginners go), I heard some people passing by.

They said, "Mom, you can save an extra $30 by watching YouTube videos on how to ski!" I initially agreed with that statement, but then I told myself that paying an extra $30 for a live instructor was the best thing I could do to pick up skiing fast.

This reminded me of Sam Ovens's quote, "The best teacher of reality is reality itself." YouTube videos work, but having a live teacher was closer to reality and would enable me to learn things even faster. After falling countless times, I eventually graduated from ski school with flying colors. I spent the next hour and a half going back and forth on a section where all the beginners were.

I was learning, but my next objective was to go on a far steeper hill with multiple turns. Right before I chickened out, I remembered that the best teacher of reality was reality itself, and the only way I would progress was to give it a shot. Long story short, I fell *hard*, but I was able to learn the following during my descent down the mountain:

- How to brake at high speeds
- How to ride a lift and get off
- How to turn at high speeds
- How to stay calm during high-stress moments
- How to safely crash

I learned all these things within a few minutes, much faster than spending hours in the beginner's section. Is there something you want to learn or improve? Remember that the best teacher of reality is reality itself.

Your Life Is Like a Car

Your life is like a car. Besides random night drives, do you hop in your car and drive without a destination? Hopefully, your answer is no to that question, but if you do, you'll quickly find out that, eventually, you'll run out of gas. Depending on the direction you're driving in, you might end up in a place that you like.

You could also end up in a place that you hate. Either of these things could be the outcome if you do not have an end destination in mind. Your life is the same way. If you live through the years and months without an end destination or goal, you may end up in a place you really like or dislike.

At the end of each year, I like to sit down and reflect on my progress. I'll write down all of my wins and failures. I'll also take time to compare the person I am at the end of the year versus when the year first began. After reflecting on the current year, I'll ask myself the following questions at the start of next year:

- What do I want to achieve this year?

- What would make this year successful?

- How can I improve (area of life)?

- How do I want to evolve this year?

By setting intention through figuring out your end destination, you take more control of your life. We will all run out of gas eventually, so control where your car will stop by defining your end destination.

22 Things I Learned

I turned 22 today. In no particular order, here are 22 things I've learned so far:

1. It is our job to ask and their job to say no

2. No one will remember your mistakes

3. Always push forward

4. The key to a long life is contrast

5. Always know when it's time to go

6. Say yes to opportunities

7. Do things today instead of tomorrow

8. Explore the world

9. Your depression is not making your life static. It's the other way around. Because your life is static, it is easy to feel depressed.

10. Money comes and goes

11. Talk to your loved ones regularly

12. Always be improving your craft

13. Goals are easy to achieve

14. Do stuff that makes you happy

15. LISTEN

16. Jesus loves you

17. Health is wealth

18. Mindset is key

19. Eat good food

20. Do things you hate doing

21. Learn to let go

22. Journal

Found something valuable in this chapter? Share it by taking a picture and tagging me on your Instagram stories @dejon_brooks!

Today's Results Came from Yesterday's Work

Today's results came from yesterday's work.

I recently bought a new camera, mic, and video setup to explore short-form content and look for new ways to go viral. I next needed to find a place to film, so I started working through my contacts to see if the owners of certain social spots would let me record videos at or outside their venues.

I received the quickest and easiest yes when I made my first call. After the owner said yes, he immediately started thanking me for promoting their weekly events without me asking for any:

- Money
- Shout-outs
- Or anything in return

My six months of acts of kindness came back around and helped me when I needed it. When I first released Trend Watchers, it took me twelve months to make my first thousand dollars. In Early January 2023, I launched the presale for a new software of mine. Thanks to the traction I already had with Trend Watchers, I was able to make my first thousand dollars within a few days.

The same thing happened with my skill set. I specifically remember reading tons of self-development books back in high school. I always ask myself, *Why am I doing this?* I was learning something new, but I didn't see any results.

I didn't let this stop me from learning, though. After years of consuming books, listening to audios, watching YouTube videos, and trying new things, I am now starting to reap the rewards of learning and stacking these skills. I noticed the same thing with my content on social media. I have so much content up; all I have to do is compile it. Once it is compiled, I can easily create books or various other digital products.

Everyone wants instant results, but no one is willing to put in the work and allow time to do its thing. Remember, today's results came from yesterday's work.

Are You Making Enough Mistakes?

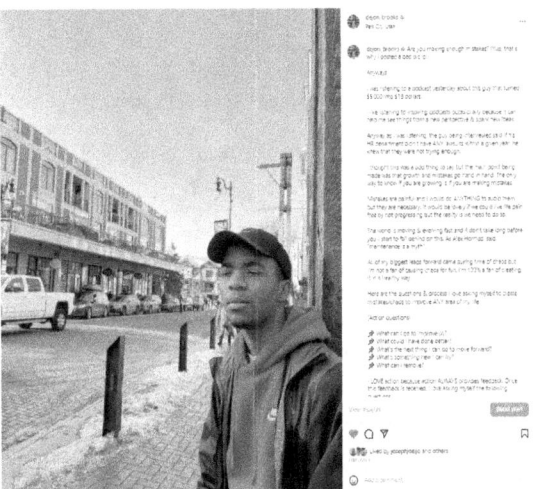

Are you making enough mistakes? (Yup, that's why I posted a bad pic.)

I was listening to a podcast about this guy who turned $5,000 into a billion dollars. I like listening to inspiring podcasts occasionally because they can help me see things from a new perspective and spark new ideas.

As I was listening, I remember the guy being interviewed said that if his HR department didn't have *any* lawsuits within a given year, he knew they were not trying enough. This was an odd thing to say, but the main point was that growth and mistakes go hand in hand. The only way to know if you are growing is if you are making mistakes.

Mistakes are painful, and I would do *anything* to avoid them, but they are necessary. It would be lovely if we could live life pain-free by not progressing, but we need to do so.

The world is moving and evolving fast, and it doesn't take long before you start to fall behind. As Alex Hormozi said, "Maintenance is a myth."

All of my most significant leaps came during a period of chaos. I'm not a fan of causing chaos for fun, but I'm 100% a fan of creating it healthily. Here are the questions and processes I love asking myself to improve *any* area of my life:

- What can I do to improve (x)?
- What could I have done better?
- What's the next thing I can do to move forward?
- What's something new I can try?
- What can I remove?

I LOVE action because action ALWAYS provides feedback. Once this feedback is received, I love asking myself the following questions:

What worked?
What didn't work?

Once this is answered, just focus on what did work and avoid what didn't work. Then, do it all over again. This is a process that doesn't only happen once. It will occur for the rest of your life, but you'll be AMAZED as to how far you'll progress within six months to a year. If you're not making mistakes or getting uncomfortable, you're not growing.

Document Everything

I'm pretty big into keeping a journal. I've been doing this religiously for the past few years. My journals are spread across Instagram (public journal) to multiple private documents that cover various aspects of my life. Some of these aspects include:

- Business
- Personal
- Relationships/dating
- Friends/family

The universe is always giving us feedback, both good and bad. A journal is a great way to keep track of events in your life and is excellent for documenting feedback. Once you have enough feedback documented, you can look over your past entries and start asking yourself:

- Why does this keep happening to me?

- Why is this always the outcome?

- For my failures, what are common occurrences that keep happening?

- For my successes, what are common occurrences that keep happening?

From my experience, asking myself these questions while reviewing my journal and past failures/successes has allowed me to discover amazing insights about myself.

It also allows me to discover the root cause of reoccurring problems, which can be life-changing. This is why I love keeping track of everything in my life. To take it to the next level, ask close people you trust, such as friends, family, or even clients:

- What could I have done better?

- What did I do wrong/right?

- Was there anything that bothered you?

I'm good at self-evaluating, but getting multiple points of view from the outside is *so* valuable; in my opinion, that's where the real growth comes from. No matter how painful the feedback is, listen and write it down. Ask lots of questions. The more, the better. If you can do this consistently, document it and review it two or three years later. You'll discover some remarkable things about yourself. I've been doing this for a long time, and it has allowed me to grow so much and turn any weakness I can discover into a strength.

The Importance of Good Friends

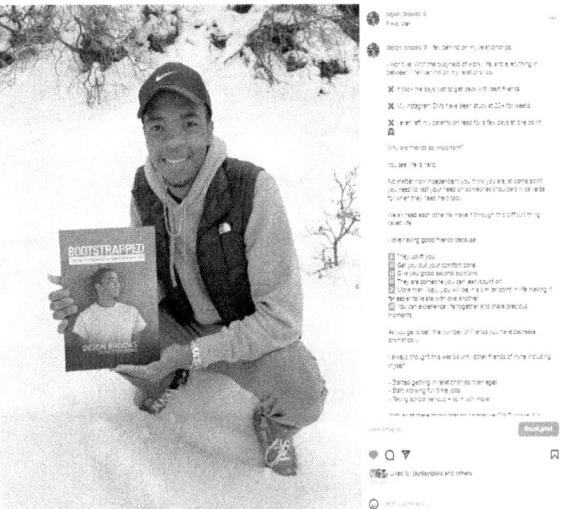

I fell behind in my relationships. I won't lie. With the busyness of work, life, and everything in between, I fell behind in my relationships. It took me days to get back with my best friends. My Instagram DMs have been stuck at 20+ for weeks. I even left my parents on read for a few days.

Why are friends so important? You see, life is hard.

No matter how independent you think you are, at some point, you need to rest your head on someone's shoulder (same for when they need help, too). We all need each other to make it through this challenging thing called life. I love having good friends because:

- They uplift you

- Get you out of your comfort zone

- Give you good second opinions

- They are someone you can lean on/count on

- You will likely be at a similar point in life, making it far easier to relate with one another.

- You can experience life together and share precious moments

As you get older, the number of friends you have decreases dramatically. I always thought this was BS until other friends of mine, including myself:

- Started getting into relationships/marriages

- Start working full-time jobs

- Taking school seriously

- Plus so much more

With all these things, it is easy to fall behind in relationships. One day turns to two, and before you know it, you've left your best friend on read for over a month. It's unbelievable how fast time flies. It's almost like trying to grab water with your bare hands. No matter how hard you try, it all just slips through your hands.

Within seconds, you gasp and go:

"How did it go by so fast?"

"Where did it go?"

"What just happened?"

"Wait, what?"

What am I trying to say?

As life gets busy, don't forget about your friends. Especially the ones that have been there through both the highs and lows. Those are the ones you want to keep the closest.

I'm grateful for my friends.

Found something valuable in this chapter? Share it by taking a picture and tagging me on your Instagram stories @dejon_brooks!

Put God First

I found the missing piece to my puzzle. I've been looking for this piece for a long time. Here's how I found it...

Around early 2023, I was doing my usual routine: doing work in my apartment, just grinding it out. I eventually felt like I needed a break, so I went to a church building near my apartment complex. In this building, they held classes all day (it was next to a major university).

I wanted to come here specifically to polish my cornhole skills. After playing cornhole for thirty minutes, I decided it was time to go. On my way out of the building, I saw a class in session with the door open, so I sat down and listened.

As you guys know, I'm always looking for ways to improve myself, and for the longest time, I couldn't find that one thing I was missing from my life. After sitting in this class for less than five minutes, it finally hit me.

I wasn't prioritizing God in my life.

I'm good at handling stuff by myself, but allowing God to lead the way makes life much more different. Not only will it help you during times of need, but something unique happens when you make God a #1 priority in your life. Your heart changes. This change of heart allows you to quickly pick up and maintain the characteristics of Christ.

These characteristics include:

- Loving
- Patient
- Forgiving
- Listener
- Caring
- Humility

Having these Christ-like attributes from making God a #1 priority in your life is a fantastic way to bless those around you. This can be:

- In your daily work
- Friends
- Family

- Relationships

Plus, so much more! This is where long-term happiness and joy are created. Are you making God a #1 priority in your life?

You Can't Please Everyone

I recently saw a video of Mr. Beast helping 1,000 blind people see again. One thousand people are a lot of people to help. If you took a look at the video, you'd expect there to be no dislikes and all positive comments.

But what happened?

Many people called him a fraud and said he did it for clout, fame, and money. I think that's unbelievable. No matter what you do and how good the intentions are (even if you're genuine), not everyone will like you.

I always knew that everyone was not going to like me. It took me a little while to get that through my thick skull, but my life improved exponentially once I learned this truth.

In what ways did my life improve? When you allow people who don't have a strong desire to be a part of your team, you end up:

- Having to do more work
- It's easier to butt heads
- It's not satisfying or fulfilling

Sometimes (for example, in business), out of desperation, you may have to suck it up and deal with these people, but that will not bring true happiness and satisfaction. True happiness and joy from others that are in your life come from them having a burning desire. I LOVE people that want to be in my life. I'm not saying they have to drop everything for me, but a little bit of desire goes a long way.

This is especially true with clients, friends, relationships, etc. The difference between these people having desire and those without is night and day. Some of my favorite benefits are:

- No BS or time-wasting games
- They genuinely care for you
- Brings real fulfillment and happiness

A few months ago, I was on a sales call with a particular prospect. This person was being cocky during the duration of our entire chat and wanted to buy to see what was up. He didn't believe in the result that our program could provide for him. He just wanted to see behind the paywall.

I could have quickly taken an easy $5k payday, but I told him no and declined his business. It was so worth not onboarding him for $5k. How much was it worth? My happiness. Sometimes you have to suck it up, but most of the time, I only deal with people with a genuine burning desire.

This goes for clients, relationships, friends, etc. Sometimes for survival, you must suck it up (primarily in business), but if you have the option, don't settle for less. Try only to deal with people who desire to join your team. I promise life will be so much more enjoyable.

Give Value at Scale

I was doing my midnight grocery shopping a few nights ago. If you've seen me shopping at midnight, I like putting my headphones in and dancing around the store while I fill up my buggy. When I reached the checkout, I needed to grab some bread, so I stepped out of line. On my way to the bread section, I complimented a guy on his outfit. This led to us having a conversation and eventually exchanging contact information for business purposes.

As I walked back to my abandoned buggy in the checkout line, I ended up sparking a conversation with the lady in front of me. I gave her a ton of value on transitioning into the tech world. We ended up exchanging socials after that interaction. Now, keep in mind, I just wanted to buy groceries and leave, but as I was making my way throughout the store, I was finding ways to ADD VALUE to other people's lives (without expecting anything in return).

I love helping other people because that is what brings true happiness. It doesn't matter if you're helping people:

- Spiritually
- Financially
- Mentally
- Emotionally

Helping people brings everlasting joy into your life. Adding value to other people's lives gets even more exciting when you figure out how to do it at scale. This is why I love social media, public speaking, and soon releasing my book (this one).

Doing these things allows me to add value to other people's lives at scale. The more people you can reach, the more fulfilled you will become.

Ask yourself, *How am I adding value to other people's lives?*

Found something valuable in this chapter? Share it by taking a picture and tagging me on your Instagram stories @dejon_brooks!

The Power of Letting Go

Our reality is a reflection of within. If the world is full of hate, your heart is probably full of hatred towards others, or the media you consume shows hate towards others.

If the world is full of opportunities and has many great people, deep down inside, you probably see the best in everyone (regardless of race, social class, or gender). I've been taking the past few weeks to really work on myself and eventually level up. I've been getting back into the concept of energy and how it can attract good or bad things into your life.

I also learned about the concept of letting go. I learned not only how to let go of people but also how to let go of expectations. When chasing a goal, we have the expectation to reach it. When it is attained, we now have the expectation to maintain that status. Chasing or maintaining an expectation brings tons of anxiety, uncertainty, and stress into your life.

By letting go of these expectations and enjoying the moment, I learned how to *really* enjoy being by myself and being grateful for what's around me. When I'm in this state of gratitude, it allows me to be naturally charismatic, happy, and optimistic. By releasing this type of energy naturally, other people can pick up on it and start gravitating in my direction.

I've been able to attract so many new friends, people to date, work opportunities, and so much more by leveraging the concept of letting go to put myself in a positive energy that attracts other positive people/opportunities. It's funny because in January 2023, I was on a call with my accountability partner, and he was tired of setting goals. He went through the month without setting any goals, and it was his best month ever. This happened all because he let go of expectations and did things in a natural way that brought opportunities to him.

If your world sucks, don't throw your fist up at it. Instead, look within and work your way from the inside out. You'll be surprised as to what can happen.

I Have the Discipline of Gods

Do you hold grudges? I was on a date recently, and the topic of patience arose. As my date and I went back and forth about the subject, she asked me if I could hold a grudge.

I thought about it for a second, and I told her yes. I can be petty and hold a grudge for years, but I choose not to do it. That negative energy in my system will completely throw me off. It won't completely throw me off center, but it's enough to take away "the spark." I don't know how to explain it, but this spark is the force that energetically draws other people to you.

Not only would it affect me in that way, but it would also affect me spiritually, professionally, and in all other areas of my life. Holding a grudge may seem insignificant, but it will affect you in ALL areas of your life. At the start of each new year, I always ask myself if there is anyone I have negative feelings towards. This includes past lovers, friends, or people I met online through a game. Thankfully, my list has been blank these past few years, but the goal is to forgive these people so you can start living your life.

Giving these people just a little bit of your energy will completely throw you off, and to be honest, you could be applying that energy towards something else more useful. Letting go of past pain can be challenging. I know some people who have been through some serious situations, but life is so much BETTER when you let go, forgive, and reclaim your energy.

Are you holding any grudges?

The Beauty of Space

Space adds beauty, meaning, and depth to our lives. In music, it is the space between the notes that create the sounds of music. Otherwise, it would just be a constant noise.

Regarding friendships, relationships, and everything else, you must give others time and space to miss you and realize what you mean to them. Doing this also allows them to enjoy their freedom and express who they are but also appreciate the gift and blessing you are to them in their lives.

When reaching our goals and ambitions, we must give that space, too. Give this enough space (mixed with a lot of action) to let things fall into place properly. As they say, Rome wasn't built in a day. Some things take time, and it's important not to rush that timeline. One Sunday, I was super stressed about my upcoming week, so I gave it space by forgetting about those problems for the rest of the day, focusing on the music and messages prepared at church, spending time with family over the phone, and just relaxing.

Humans love to fill in space. If you buy a TV, game console, or car, you will use it. You'll eventually buy a fish if you get an empty fish bowl. If a room in your apartment is empty, you'll eventually fill it up. If the car is quiet, you'll turn the music on. Learning the art of adding meaningful space is not easy, but it will make your life much better and more enjoyable.

Found something valuable in this chapter? Share it by taking a picture and tagging me on your Instagram stories @dejon_brooks!

Stay in Your Lane

The grass is greener where you water it, so stay in your lane. I recently went to a real estate conference, and I learned a lot of stuff. Not only did I learn a lot about real estate, but I also learned a lot about what I *don't* want to do for a career.

The first guy that spoke was a lawyer; let me tell you, he knew his stuff. He probably got paid tons of money to represent his construction clients, but the thought of doing all that legal work, dealing with the government, and paperwork left me depressed and with a massive headache.

After lunch, one of the leading real estate developers (multifamily) went into the construction update of each project. Sure, he was making a ton of money building these buildings, but every ongoing project had some drama. This drama includes:

- City councils being funny

- MASSIVE unexpected expenses

- Builders taking shortcuts, prolonging deadlines, and increasing costs

Don't get me wrong, I love real estate, and I'm going to get into it soon, but as far as doing construction management, I will stay far away. The upside is incredible, but in my opinion, managing the projects wouldn't make me happy. I'd rather be an investor and be hands-off. Now, I'm not writing this chapter to be bitter. I'm writing it because I was able to learn two things.

1) No matter what I'm going through, someone else has a bigger problem.

2) Focus on your craft and stick to it. Mine is marketing. Just because someone makes more money doing something else doesn't mean you should bounce around to the next shiny object.

All career paths in life are hard, and you will experience setbacks. The best thing you could do is identify what you love doing the most and spend years polishing your craft. As they say, the grass is greener where you water it.

Final Thoughts

Everything you read between the first chapter and now occurred between 2020 and 2023. During this period, I moved 1,000+ miles from my hometown, grew a tech company with my own money, and learned how to transition from a boy to a man.

As I was going through this journey, I made it a priority to document my journey. Not only did documenting my journey help me clear my thoughts, but it allowed me to do the following...

Find direction

Many times during this period, I felt like giving up. Yes, I had things going for myself, but sometimes it felt like nothing would work at times.

Whenever I felt like this, I would grab some food, drive up a mountain, and write for 30–60 minutes. I like calling these mini-thinking trips. If you read the book all the way through, you'll know exactly what these are. Combining thinking trips with journaling allowed me to find direction even when there seemed no other way to go.

Find purpose through sharing my story

I have two sets of journals. I have a private one and a public one. I maintained a public one for fun, but as time went on, it started getting attention. Before I knew it, people started sending me messages and emails about how my journey inspired them to start theirs or motivated them to keep pushing.

This accidental by-product of documenting my journey publicly has given me a natural purpose of helping others by documenting my wins and failures.

Stay positive no matter how tough times get

No matter how good your life is, it will eventually become hard. Being able to go back and read previous journal entries has given me the strength to endure whatever I may be going through at the time. To succeed in life, you must always get back up after getting knocked down. Having this track record to refer back to makes it easier to get back up when life knocks you down.

As I close out this book, I want to challenge you to start documenting your journey publically. You can do this by:

- Starting a blog
- Running an email list
- Starting a YouTube channel
- Doing workshops/public speaking
- Create short-form content
- Write a book
- Plus, so much more!

Even if you only have 1,000 followers, do it. No matter what you talk about, it will help someone.

Out of 1,000 people, if you spoke about having financial issues, a tiny percentage of your audience will be able to relate directly to what you're going through.

Same thing if you were to talk about losing a loved one, going through a breakup, or anything. Someone within your audience will be able to relate with you directly. It all comes down to timing, but it's YOUR job to take action by sharing your story first.

The Next Step

I help individuals and organizations tell their stories online to go viral and build communities. If you are interested in working with me, here are the different ways you can reach me:

Speaking

Want me to speak to your team or event?

https://presellyourstory.com/speaking

Coaching

For all of my available coaching programs

https://presellyourstory.com/coaching

Social media

Join my email list for weekly golden nuggets.

https://presellyourstory.com/dejon

Workshop Notes